Your Unstoppable Brand

The practical guide to engaging your ideal
customers through the power of stories

Janet Wentworth

10X group

The 10X Group | Santa Rosa, California

Your Unstoppable Brand: The practical guide to engaging your ideal customers through the power of stories

Published by:

The 10X Group
645 Fourth Street, Suite 212
Santa Rosa, CA 95404

Email: janet.wentworth@gmail.com
www.unstoppablebrand.com
Unstoppable Brand™ of Janet Wentworth

First published in 2013

ISBN: 978-0-9895309-0-3

Printed in the United States of America

DISCLAIMER
This book is designed to provide small business owners with a process and ideas to improve their marketing by using business stories. Topics covered are not exhaustive but are designed to supplement existing resources. The author and publisher make no representations or warranties and assume no liabilities of any kind with the respect to the accuracy or completeness of the content of this book or its suitability for any particular business. Unless otherwise specifically stated, the views are those of the author. Readers assume responsibility for their use of the information and ideas presented.

Acknowledgement

I would like to thank the following who have made this book possible.

Kendall Haven for writing *Story Proof: The Science Behind the Startling Power of Story* which opened the door to my own journey into stories and provided me with an understanding of the scientific foundation to the power of stories.

My many clients who have proven the need for stories in their marketing efforts and have worked on writing their own stories.

The attendees in my workshops who encouraged me through support and feedback, and taught me so much about what was needed in this book.

The authors who graciously gave permission to include their stories: Michael S. Malone, Sean D'Souza, Kerry Rego, Neal Gottleib, Boku Kadama, John Jantsch, Marcus Stout, and Robert Bruce.

A special thank you to Rachel Meserve for persevering through the first storytelling workshop and contributing so much insightful feedback for improving the book and the course.

This book would not have happened without the family support of my son, John, for his feedback and technical support, and my husband, Patrick, for his unflagging dedication in reviewing drafts, checking URLs and other details, and supporting me through this long process.

Preface

Jennifer was sitting in my office while I listened to a repeat of what I had heard so many times before: "I have no money to hire a web developer or a graphic artist. I do everything myself. I have a homemade web site using mostly photos I have taken. I don't have enough money for a true shopping cart so I have people email me when they want to buy something. I have great products that have some loyal customers. I just don't have enough customers. But if I can't get sales up, I can't afford to really promote my business. If I can't afford to promote my business, I can't increase sales. I am trapped!"

These were the conversations I used to dread. I could help people improve their web sites (as long as they had someone to do the work). I could advise them on how to get better search engine visibility, how to improve their use of Facebook, how to start a Google AdWords campaign, or any number of other online marketing ideas. We could improve their performance at trade shows or farmers markets. We could talk about direct mail or joining networking groups.

But all of this takes money to get started, and Jennifer, like so many before her, had no budget for any of these ideas. Her business-on-a-shoestring was stalled with no solution.

She did have several things in her favor. I could tell that Jennifer had a good natural eye for design. Her product hang tags were attractive with an elegant feel, but sadly, visually disjointed from her web site design. Her product photos were quite good, despite her lack of professional product photography skills or dedicated lighting setup.

Most importantly, she was very passionate about her business. She raised specialty sheep and sold the raw wool to weavers. She also handcrafted a variety of wool products. I could tell from the photos that the sheep were beloved. There was something in her voice that convinced me she had an inner fire for her sheep and her business. I also knew she had a story to tell.

I had been reading about the power of stories, the latest brain research into stories, why people are attracted to brands, and how consumers make their buying decisions. The more I read, the more fascinated I became with the science behind stories and the opportunities stories brought to the small business owner.

Rather than spending time helping clients find free web hosting or low cost logo design services, we could start investing time in what really mattered: getting ideal customers attracted and engaged. True engagement with ideal customers is far more valuable than a pretty web site.

Being able to tell your story is truly empowering. I have watched as clients grew from meek (I have this little business . . .) to confident. They don't just tell their story, they truly believe it.

They have learned stories are not just tools for marketing, they are tools for changing their beliefs about themselves and their businesses.

For Jennifer, it is her story that will enable her to grow a business despite her lack of funding. Her stories (of course, there are stories for each of her sheep, as well as each of her products) will engage her ideal customers. Those customers will spread her stories. They will visit her web site and Facebook page and will smile while reading about a new lamb being born or a new product being developed.

When she goes to the craft fairs and farmers markets, she will engage the shoppers with her stories. People will stop by just for an update on the animals.

Eventually she will be able to hire someone to enhance her web site or perhaps she can start using a shopping cart to make online buying easier. These things will come as her stories spread, and as her fans grow in number and loyalty.

Jennifer is learning the power of stories to build her business.

As a small business owner, regardless of size or budget, you can do the same. **Stories are free. Stories are already inside you. All you need to do is get them out!**

Are you ready to start your story journey?

Janet Wentworth

Contents

INTRODUCTION

brand
stories
marketing

customer expectations + values
promotion + pricing + positioning + placement

Does This Sound Like You?

Are you like Jennifer in the Preface? You have great enthusiasm for your business and your customers, but your marketing is lackluster. Your print brochures and web site lack personality. They lack a clear demonstration of the passion you have for why you are in this business. There is little consistency in your marketing materials. You may have several variations of your logo, brochures do not look like your business card, and your web site uses a generic design theme. Your business is not attracting the right customers or enough customers.

You know in your heart you have something of value to offer. You are passionate about your business. Why is it so hard to communicate this passion to your prospects and customers?

You need some magic to bring in new customers and keep previous customers returning.

Stories can be that magic for your business
The rest of this book will help you learn why and how this magic works, but first we need to step back and review the history of buyers and marketers.

Marketing Then and Now

We live in the best of times and the worst of times, at least as far as being consumers and business owners. Never in the history of mankind have we consumers had so many choices. Not just choices of which grocery store to patronize or which brand of car to buy. We have choices in innovative, never-even-imagined-before products like iPads, bungee-jumping adventures, and turn-back-the-clock cosmetic treatments.

This abundance creates extraordinary opportunities for the small business owner. Buyers have unprecedented disposable income to spend, and we, as owners, have the opportunity to promote specific offerings to help them spend it.

But the abundance also has a dark side. With so many choices facing buyers, how do they decide what to buy and from whom to buy? What can we do to attract the right customers? How can our businesses stand out from the noise in our constantly expanding online and offline marketplaces?

Back in those fondly remembered "good old days," if we needed groceries, there was only one choice: the corner grocery. It had a complete range of products (a laughably small range by today's standards), and we could just walk home with our purchases.

Today, depending on our affluence, we worry about the carbon footprint of the store, if we should use paper or plastic, if the lettuce is organic, if child labor packed the cereal box, if those soybeans were genetically modified.

We also worry about buying the right brands. Will my friends be impressed with this trendy new ingredient? Do I feel better about myself because I support fair trade causes? Does that grocery offer products to fit with my vegetarian, vegan, gluten-free, or Paleolithic diet?

As a business owner, is there any hope to survive in such a disjointed and fractured marketplace?

The good news is that you can do better than survive, you can thrive. **Even the smallest solo entrepreneur can become an Unstoppable Brand**. But, it means a shift in your marketing mindset.

NOTES

What Is an Unstoppable Brand?

Have you ever experienced a bit of juicy gossip making the rounds of your office? How about an email with a hilarious story? Do you remember stories from your childhood, such as *Aesop's Fables* or *Where the Wild Things Are* or *The Little Engine That Could*? Of course you do. Why? Because they are stories, and stories are Unstoppable! **Our brains are built to listen for stories, and they make it almost impossible to ignore them.**

Once you learn how, you can use the power of stories to make your business thrive. Stories are most powerful when they are heard by your ideal customers. Using stories, you attract the right customers—those who love what you offer and will become loyal customers. They are excited about your business and will refer their friends. No more trying to market to everyone hoping for a small return on your investment.

Stories are easy for you to use, even if you consider yourself a reluctant marketer. Your stories will be easy for your customers to share with their friends and colleagues. They are free to be spread and to be shared. They have wings and lives of their own.

Just like those viral cat videos, your stories, and thus your business, become Unstoppable.

A Few Definitions

The terms brand, branding, and marketing have evolved over time and can have multiple meanings. So before we get too far along, it is a good time to define our terms. Please read the four boxes on the next page so you understand the definitions we will be using in this book.

Brand + Branding

Phase 1 = Brand Ownership
I Own This

The word brand, from an old Norse word for burn, has been used in English since the 12th century. It became identified with products from its use by cattlemen in the Old West: to burn a unique mark on their cattle to tell them apart.

The goal of the brand mark was to distinguish my products from yours and to avoid fights over ownership.

Phase 2 = Brand Differentiation
Please Buy My Brand

With the Industrial Revolution and the rise of manufactured goods, multiple companies were producing the same products, like soap. They could ship their soap around the country. No longer was the local soap maker the only choice.

To provide product differentiation, companies built on their brand marks with fancy names, slogans, jingles, etc., to make their "brand" stand out in the mind of the consumer.

By the 1950s, the rise of the consumer (with less time and more discretionary income) was paralleled by the rise of the big marketing agency (with its big budget). Using every possible marketing trick to make the product stand out in the minds of the consumer became known as branding. With so much competition in the marketplace, branding became a major force, especially for the behemoth consumer packaged goods industry. Marketers began "brand awareness" advertising, where there might be no product mentioned in the ad. Its sole purpose was to drill the name into the mind of the consumer.

Phase 3 = Brand Promise
Do you love me?

Branding has evolved from the basic identification elements of color, logo, and tag line to the creation of an experience that fulfills the customer's expectations.

That evolution has shifted ownership of the brand to the customer. Thanks to online sites like Yelp, customers now decide what your brand is. Does the brand expectation you promise meet the customer's reality?

How does brand promise work? Consider Tiffany vs. Costco. They both sell jewelry, but their brand promises are quite different.

Costco offers a large range of jewelry in the low- to mid-price range in their warehouse locations with no jewelry experts to help with your selection. You see what you like, ask for it from the locked case, and then stand in the grocery line to pay for it.

Tiffany is a high end merchant with stores in exclusive shopping districts. The stores are elegantly appointed and often have security guards at the front door. The jewelry is the finest quality with unique designs and high-end price tags. Offer your loved one a present in the signature Tiffany blue box and you will get quite a different reaction than if you brought home a piece of jewelry packed with 20 lbs. of dog kibble and a gallon of mayonnaise.

Costco customers are happy with the self-service approach, affordable prices, and no sales pressure.

Tiffany's customers crave the high-end experience, ego boost, and satisfaction that they have bought from the best. If Tiffany were to start having midnight madness sales or move into a local strip mall, their promise would be broken.

Marketing

Marketing encompasses all the ways you communicate the value of your products and services to the marketplace through the traditional 4 Ps of pricing, promotion, placement, and positioning

Marketing includes your store location, advertising, distribution channels, Facebook page, email signature, and more.

All your marketing efforts need to support the brand promise you make to your ideal customers JC Penney is a good example of a company that suffered from a new marketing strategy when it abandoned its brand promise and disappointed its ideal customers.

A new CEO felt that offering a simpler pricing structure would attract more customers as he felt the mashup of weekend-only events, daily-only events, in-store, and online specific sales was too confusing.

Unfortunately, he misunderstood his customers. They are extremely price sensitive. They like the thrill of snagging a great deal. They relish the ritual of visiting JC Penney for the special sales. They love clipping coupons. JC Penney with its new marketing tactics, failed to meet the expectations of its loyal customers and paid the price with its dismal sales numbers. The highly regarded CEO is now an ex-CEO because he failed to understand his ideal customers and broke his brand promise.

In this book, we will use the term marketing to cover all you do to communicate with your customers. The term branding will include marketing efforts designed to create the impression you want and to set the stage for your customers' experience. Ultimately, however, your brand is in the hands of the marketplace.

Stories

Stories are the emotional component of your marketing activities. They engage your ideal customers and are the bridge between your marketing and your brand.

Stories allow you to go beyond features and benefits, low prices, and generic sounding products. Customers have evolved from merely buying commodities; they want to buy from companies that they like and trust. They want to support companies that share their values and they identify with. Stories allow you to express those values.

How do you use stories? In countless ways. Replace that tired timeline of your company history with a story of your founding. For staff bios, don't just think in terms of awards and education, tell us about each person's inner passion and dreams. Testimonials can go from just vague "atta boys" to real stories of overcoming problems, or avoiding disaster, by using your product. Stories allow you to share your work in the local community or with causes around the world.

Stories do not replace your current marketing efforts, they will become part of it.

They make your marketing more memorable, more engaging, more personal, and more effective.

This isn't just some wishful thinking. The power of stories is based on solid scientific research into how we think, how we make decisions, and how we store information.

Humans have been telling each other stories for thousands of years. Now you can harness this power of how we respond to stories to create a loyal following of your ideal customers.

Lets Be Clear: Goals of this Book

Learn why stories are critical

Before you can put stories to work for maximum impact, you need to understand why they are so persuasive. Once you understand the Unstoppable power of stories, you will become a story evangelist. Chapter 2 will introduce you to why stories are so important.

Learn how to write good stories

Crafting stories isn't difficult, but there are techniques to help you develop your story chops. Whether you are telling verbal stories or crafting written stories, you need to know the critical elements of a story and how to make your story believable and interesting.

Knowing how to write a story is every bit as important as knowing where to use your stories for effective marketing.

Learn how to use stories to resonate with your ideal customers and nurture your brand

Using your stories correctly will attract your ideal customers. No more marketing to the world-at-large. Your stories will be on the right frequency for your ideal customers.

Learn how to incorporate your stories into your marketing efforts

Your marketing needs to get people to know, like, and trust you. Once you have stories written, what exactly do you do with them? We will be covering the ways you can build a library of stories, plus how to use them in your individual marketing activities. We will also discuss how to support your stories with visual elements for a cohesive presentation.

Develop habits to keep your story crafting going

Story-based marketing is only useful if it becomes second nature to you. It isn't enough to add a few stories to your web site and quit. You must develop habits that enable you to see story opportunities whenever they appear.

Getting the Most from this book

The goal of this book is to get you working on stories, on seeing the value of stories, and of knowing when and how to use stories in your marketing as quickly as possible. It is an instruction manual and a workbook

The inner columns of many pages are ruled so you can take notes as you read.

I came from a family with a deep reverence for books. Dad had collected books on Western Americana since he was a teenager. Every book was encased in a library-quality book cover to protect the dust jacket. Every book was entered in his card catalog (we are talking old fashioned index cards here) and its condition noted. We were allowed to read the books, but only with the utmost care. No dirty hands. No paperclips or dog-eared corners. No notes in the margins.

Those were deeply ingrained lessons, and even today I cannot bring myself to write in a book. **But this book is different!** This book is yours to write in, dog ear, add sticky notes to. Carry it around and spill coffee on it. Use it. Love it. Learn from it.

Do not skip around

The chapters are in a logical sequence, so work through each chapter in order.

The sequence is:
1. Learn why stories are important
2. Learn the four critical elements of a story
3. Write an initial story
4. Define your ideal customer
5. Learn about archetypes and find yours
6. Continue writing stories while you verify they will engage your ideal customer and stay true to your archetype
7. Learn advanced techniques to improve your writing
8. Decide how to use stories in your marketing for a solid story-based brand
9. Develop a story habit

Exercise Boxes

When you see a box like this, it means it is an exercise to do before moving on to further reading.

Reading is good, but **doing is the only way to develop the story habit** and to write great stories. The exercises in these boxes are designed to help you build your "story muscles." Don't skip over them.

If you want to learn more about how to develop your writing skills as efficiently and as deeply as possible, read *The Talent Code: Greatness Isn't Born. It's Grown. Here's How.* by Daniel Coyle.

Along the way, examples of other brands and how they use stories will illustrate the points. Learning from others will help you progress faster.

This is a hands-on process that you can do alone or with a group. If you know other marketers, start a mastermind group of your own so you can learn from, and support, each other.

Write as much as you can

There are specific writing exercises in the book, but these are only the bare minimum. You should be writing every day. Get a notebook and write down all your ideas for stories and where to use them. Note marketing stories that others are using.

Developing story muscles

Throughout this book there will be exercises to help develop your story muscles. Becoming a good marketing storyteller is more than understanding stories, you must practice your skills until they become second nature.

Think of a jazz musician. She must practice the scales until playing them becomes an ingrained skill. There is no time to stop and think "What key is this?" or "What is the best chord for this melody?" or "What is that chord progression that guitarist is playing?"

She doesn't have to stop and think because through years of practice she knows (and her fingers know) how the music works.

Your goal is to build your story muscles in the same fashion. Fortunately, although becoming a master storyteller can be a lifetime process, you have a head start over the beginning jazz musician. You already know how to recognize a story and have the necessary language skills to create your own stories. Just start now and keep practicing.

A Few Words Before You Begin

Story journal

Carrying a paper notebook, a smartphone with dictation ability, or another method you prefer to keep track of your ideas is a necessity. Ideas will come at the least opportune times. Don't let these ideas get away! I use my camera phone to take photos of signs and storefronts for inspiration, even on vacation. Great inspiration is all around you, but without recording it you will probably forget it.

See the Story Journal box to the right for getting started with your story journal.

Storytelling vs. story writing

Storytelling is the verbal telling of a story and is different than a written story. With a spoken story you may use intonation, vocal dynamics, body language, maybe even props. Spoken stories will change with the audience and the situation.

Written stories just have the words. You don't have the opportunity to revise the story to fit each audience so the story used in your written materials, such as a brochure, is static until you rewrite the brochure. You must use all your writing powers to create drama and interest without getting any feedback from the reader.

Even though these are different ways to communicate a story, for simplicity in this book, we will be using the word storytelling to cover both written and verbal stories.

Feedback

Seek feedback on your stories. Start telling them immediately and see how they work. Especially seek out people who will give you honest feedback. Friends and relatives may just say "good job!" and not offer useful feedback.

Instead, try telling stories in business situations and watch the reactions. Your listener will let you know if you have hit the mark.

Story Journal

If you are serious about developing a library of story ideas, turning those ideas into stories, keeping track of story opportunities, and really turning your marketing into an Unstoppable Brand, you need to develop the story journal habit.

This can be a small notebook, a smartphone with a dictation app, a dedicated recording device, or a combination of any of these tools. The method isn't important; the habit of recording your ideas is.

What goes in your story journal?

Everyday events like customer compliments, customer complaints, training issues, and other routine business events all have story potential.

Non-business events can serve as a catalyst for creative thinking. If you stay with your mind always focused on your business and your industry, you will miss some of life's greatest inspirations.

For example, I was listening to the radio when a journalist started talking about how flowers attract bees. It was a natural fit for the chapter on defining ideal customers. You will read more about this in Chapter 4. If I only listened to business news channels, I would have missed this insightful analogy.

Developing Story Muscles

So many people feel overworked that "I'm too busy" has become a very convenient and readily acceptable excuse for not having the time to do something new. But successful storytellers never rest, as stories are a way of life, not an item on a to-do list. Storytellers are always looking for ideas, inspiration, role models, and also missed opportunities. They make time to hone their craft.

So what can you do **right now** to improve your story crafting skills without having to carve out precious time from your already packed schedule? Develop your story muscles by taking advantage of situations where you can do a little creative multi-tasking!

- While standing in the check-out line, you can pick one product at random and answer the question "What story are they telling?"
- Take that same product and think of several other options for that story. Come up with outrageous ideas.
- What visuals, colors, tone of voice, and other elements reinforce the story? Do you have ways to improve the visuals?
- Driving to work, pick a business as you pass by and think about any stories they tell. If they have no stories, what could they do to add stories to their marketing?
- While waiting for an appointment to start, think of a business partner or vendor who is not using any stories and make up a fictitious story for them. How could they resonate with their ideal customers?
- Where else can you find a few minutes to do a few story calisthenics?

Resources

Telling stories and using stories in marketing have become very popular topics lately. There are many great books written on why we are attracted to stories and why they are so important to marketers. Check out Chapter 10 for book recommendations to deepen your understanding of stories.

Avoid These Common Myths

Despite the clear value in using stories, many people avoid them. It may be that they just haven't thought about the value of stories, but often it is an unfounded, but strongly held, bias against stories. Here are some of the most common misconceptions.

Myth #1 | Stories are for kids

Yes, children love stories, and we have all told stories to children and listened to stories as children. But that does not mean stories are childish and not useful for adults in business situations.

According to Kendall Haven in *Story Proof, the Science Behind the Startling Power of Story*, "Humans have told, used and relied on stories for over 100,000 years." These were not kids' stories, but stories used for man's survival in a dangerous world. It doesn't get more serious than survival!

Myth #2 | Stories are not for B2B selling

We have all heard it: to market you need facts. You need lists of features and benefits. People buy based on logic. You might sell on emotion to a consumer, but business buyers want hard facts. All of this is wrong.

Selling to a business is still selling to people. They don't change their brain biology when they walk through the office door. True, there may be more people involved in a business decision. The sales cycle may be longer, and you may have more competitors. But it still comes down to selling to people who are hardwired for story.

In fact, stories can give you the edge in a business setting. As there will be multiple people involved in the sales cycle, using stories, which are so easy to share, ensures that your message gets out as you intended. You won't have to worry that your contact forgot your list of features; she will remember your stories.

You can create variations of your stories specifically for the CEO, the plant manager, or anyone else you interact with during your sales process.

Myth #3 | You are born a storyteller or not

We all know people who are great storytellers. They seem to have the gift. Perhaps you feel that you don't, and that is that. No stories for you!

Don't sell yourself short. You just need a little help getting started. Have you ever told someone about your vacation? Or told your children about your own childhood? Then you have told a story.

Usually, the stories we tell just happen without our thinking about them. But to create stories for your business, you will want so learn techniques that allow you to create stories for specific needs.

Most of your stories will be written and will be used on your web site, in brochures, flyers, and newsletters. But spoken stories will have their place as well.

You may never stand up in front of an audience, like Jerry Seinfeld and hold an audience's attention for 60 minutes. You don't need to. That is not what we are talking about. Jerry is an entertainer. Once you learn the basic elements of a story and a few techniques, you will be creating and delivering your marketing stories with confidence.

Myth #4 | Stories are for extroverts

This is one of the most satisfying myths to bust. Story-based marketing is such a gift to the introvert. You no longer have to feel that you need to be bragging, beating your chest, and shouting to the world how fabulous you, your products, and your services are. You don't need audacious stories or to seek the limelight with your dramatic presentations. Your stories will demonstrate your message far more eloquently than any "hey look at me" speech. Besides, many of your stories will have your customer as the hero. You can stay quietly in the background.

Myth #5 | You have to be a good writer

If you are thinking you need to be Stephen King, don't worry. That isn't the kind of writing skill you need. You do need basic English skills. A good thesaurus wouldn't hurt. What you really need are practice, patience, and feedback.

Most of your stories will be quite short, perhaps only a paragraph or two. Others will be longer. But, you won't be doing character development, inventing sub plots, or needing the wit of George Bernard Shaw.

Your stories will be authentic, honest, and from the heart. They will be crafted to resonate with your ideal customers who need what you are selling. Those qualities you can't learn or buy.

Myth #6 | Stories are for my *About Us* page

Yes, your *About Us* page will probably have a story, but that is only the beginning. Every one of your testimonials should be a story. Your mission statement might be a story. You will need stories to answer questions when you are in a sales call. You will have written stories, spoken stories, formal stories, and ad hoc stories. Once you start writing stories for your brand, you will think of more and more ways to use them.

Myth #7 | Stories are fiction

Robert McKee, famed author and screenwriter, says, "What happens is fact, not truth. Truth is what we think about what happens."

The stories we will be writing are truthful and do need to be honest. However, stories you write will not be documentaries. You will tell a story for a reason and will only include the factual details that are needed to convey your message. But that doesn't make them fiction.

Even if you write a story about creative ways to use a product from the perspective of a fictional customer, it is still truth. The story will represent the experience of other, real customers.

Myth #8 | Stories are for simple lessons

Far from being only for simple lessons, stories may be best used as a way to cover a complex topic that otherwise would be lost in the facts and technical information. Stories free the listener from being burdened by the details and the complexities. Instead they are open to the "big picture"—your message.

It is true that stories are not the best method for writing a catalytic converter troubleshooting guide. Stories need to be used appropriately.

Stories are used to teach a lesson, convey a message, encourage action, and prove a point.

Myth #9 | I don't have any stories

Trust me, you have stories. In Chapter 3 we will discuss how to find material for your stories.

NOTES

WHY MARKETING STORIES?

Why Stories Are Important

The human brain is hardwired for story. As Kendall Haven states in his book *Story Proof: the Science Behind the Startling Power of Story*, "One hundred thousand years of human reliance on story has evolutionarily rewired the human brain to be predisposed to think in story terms and to use story structure to create meaning and to make sense of events and others' actions."

The Epic of Gilgamesh, one of the earliest surviving examples of a written story, was written in cuneiform on clay tablets by 2500 BCE. By this time there was a well-established oral tradition of storytelling. This human focus on stories continues in an unbroken line to master screenwriters and novelists who entertain, educate, and inspire us with their works, as well as today's parents who tell stories of their own childhood experiences.

All of these stories continue to intensify our story-focused brains. Stories have helped us share experiences, learn from them, and prepare for new experiences. This is how it has been since we were avoiding saber-toothed tigers, and it is still true today. This is why our brains are wired to be on the alert for stories and pay attention to them.

Just think—all those hours spent listening to Dr. Seuss as a child were not just for fun, you were really training your brain! For the marketer, this story-wired brain provides a proven path into the thought processes of your ideal customers.

Chapter 10 has resources if you wish to explore this fascinating topic of current research into brain biology and evolution of the human brain

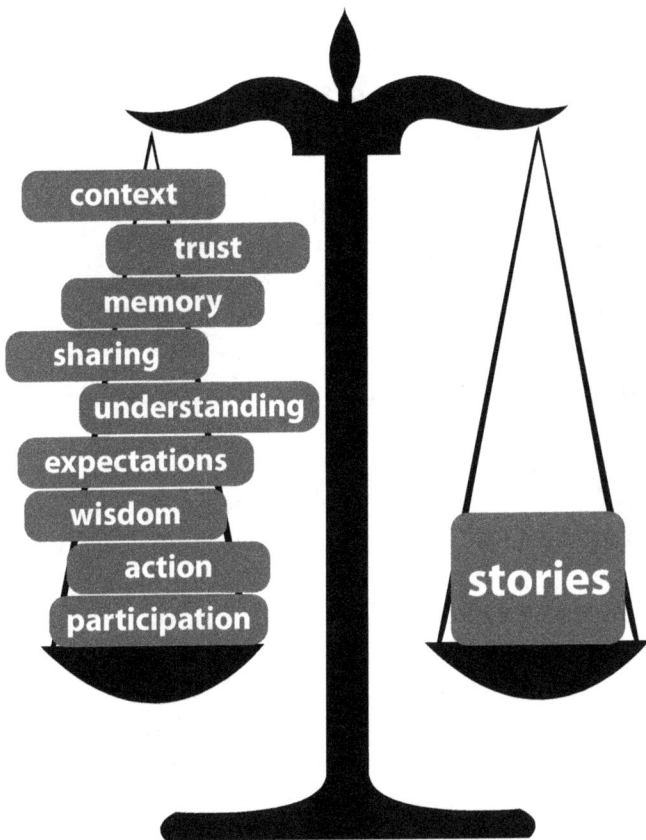

What does this mean to you, the marketer?
Understanding the power of stories completely changes how you look at marketing. You now know that relying solely on facts, features, and benefits is not the way to engage your ideal customers and persuade them to buy.

You also know that you don't need to trick, connive or sweet talk prospects. You don't need to bribe them with low prices, coupons, etc.* If she is your ideal customer, your story will do the job of engaging her.

Rather than looking at marketing as a creative, expensive, and possibly mysterious process, you can be confident a story-based brand will bring you business success.

* (NOTE—This does not mean you never offer discounts or other incentives. It does mean that these tactics no longer have to be your primary sales tactics. They can be useful tools, but will never be the main reason loyal customers buy from you.)

The benefits of marketing stories

Stories make it easier to develop marketing materials
Ever struggle with what to write on your blog? Are your Facebook posts not getting any love from likes, shares, or comments? When you start to develop a new ad, flyer, or customer promotion do you feel you are always at a loss for ideas? If the answers are yes, then you are probably not using the power of story-based branding.

After you have learned how to use stories and developed your writing skills, you will find that creating marketing materials is easier and more satisfying.

Stories let the listener participate
Current studies of the brain show that when you listen to a story your brain reacts just as if you were actually experiencing it. The old advice to "paint a picture" for your listener implies a passive role for that listener. The reality is their brains are every bit as involved as if they had actually experienced it.

I came from a reading family. I always had at least one book in progress, usually historical fiction. Early on I noticed that I was always sad when the book ended. I felt like I had lost a good friend. So I started reading longer and longer books. 750 pages might be good, but 1000 pages were better. That gave me more time to stay immersed in the story.

At the time, I had no idea that I was even choosing books for this reason. Then one day I finished reading Edna Ferber's *Giant*. I was crushed. That story was the doorway to people and places so unlike my own. I had never been to Texas or seen a cattle ranch or an oil well. The family rivalry, the bigotry, the greed were all foreign to me. But I was entranced with this other world and didn't quite know how to react when it was over. I was in a fog for days after the book ended.

I knew they weren't real people, but they seemed so alive to me. Why did I feel this way after a story? It was just words on a page (or images on a movie screen). What else was going on?

I was experiencing what neuroscientists have proven: that I was not just reading the story, I was experiencing it! This is good news for me, as now I don't feel like such a fool when feeling so lost after each season's end of Downton Abbey.

Each reader will create her unique mental images based on her experience. Your job is to stimulate the imagination of your audience. Beware, however, that if you do not include enough of the important details you want the reader to remember, she will provide her own. Your story may morph into something unintended.

Stories attract attention
Picture yourself at work walking down the hall to the copy machine. You pass by someone, hear " . . . then I learned that Joe . . ." and you slow down. You have just been hooked by a story.

A story catches your attention so that it is almost impossible to not stop and listen. With other marketing efforts you have to work hard to get attention, but stories are like magnets. If your ideal customer is within earshot, her brain won't let her ignore your story.

Stories create meaning, understanding, and context in the listener's mind

One way to create a memorable story is to include elements that are already familiar to the reader.

If you are offering a weight loss program, then your story includes information about weight loss, the struggles people have with losing weight and/or keeping it off, weight loss techniques they may have tried, and other information familiar to most people looking to lose weight. Then your story will include how someone has lost weight (despite all these past problems) using your solution.

By providing context (their weight loss struggles) to the story, the reader is immediately engaged. If, on the other hand, you immediately began a deep discussion on the biochemistry of your miracle supplement, most people would be lost. They have no understanding of what you are saying and will not be interested.

Stories are easier to remember (and are more accurately remembered) than just facts

Because our brains store information in story format, information fed to it as a story, with all the story elements, makes it easy to store and easy to recall. Lists of facts will be forgotten almost immediately.

Stories are easy to share

We love to tell stories, and your story will be easy for your customers to share with their friends. They are ready-made for social media sharing!

Stories are containers for wisdom

There is a widely-quoted tale, perhaps apocryphal, that in the early days of Nordstorm department store a "customer" came in to return a pair of snow tires that he didn't want. This was the Fairbanks, Alaska store, but Nordstrom sold clothing, not tires and never has sold tires. Yet the sales clerk gave the customer a refund.

Did this episode really happen? Who knows? There are differing accounts. One plausible version is that the Nordstrom building previously was used by a tire store, and the customer may have just been confused. But that isn't the point. The value of this story is to show how much latitude a Nordstrom employee has in keeping a customer satisfied. They don't need a company policy detailing specific situations that can be handled by a sales person on the floor, a chart of approved refund allowances, or how to escalate a problem up the chain of command. This story says it all.

Stories can also work as wisdom sharing devices when dealing with prospects in sales situations. We tend to believe in the overriding power of numbers and facts. But, a customer success story may be a more effective way to overcome objections and make the sale.

Stories are integral to human activities

Stories have been told through the ages to help others learn to avoid danger (like saber-toothed tigers and poisonous plants), how to get along, cultural norms, family values, tribal/national/family history, and ramifications of inappropriate behavior. We already know that we learn through stories, so your marketing stories are just exploiting a well-used path.

Stories let your deeds talk for you

Many people are not natural promoters. They are more private, reserved, and not comfortable bragging about themselves, their services, or their products. Stories are the perfect vehicle in these situations.

Don't brag, just tell a story! You don't even have to be in the story (well, you probably want to be in your *About Us* story). Use your customers as your story characters. Let them be the heroes.

Stories get people to act

Have you noticed that whenever there is a major disaster (earthquake, fire, or home foreclosure crisis) the news story will begin by describing a single victim. Why?

Journalists know a story will get your attention and keep you reading, while a list of the tragic statistics will only encourage you to find another article. They also know that it is likely to get you to act, possibly sending money to the victim or a relief organization. Nobody sends donations to the U.S. Bureau of Labor Statistics!

If the article had been a factual presentation of fire losses in the local area for the past year and dollar value of possessions lost, no one would even think about helping. Why not? There is no story, no people to identify with, no overcoming obstacles. There is no reason to care.

Stories are entertainment and instruction

We all love to be entertained. Why else are crazy cat videos so popular on YouTube? Stories have a built-in entertainment value, which makes your message, even for serious products and business services, so much more interesting.

Stories defeat the Curse of Knowledge

We have all been there: explaining the great features and benefits to a prospect, but they just don't seem to get it. We know that what we are offering is perfect for their situation, but we can't seem to get that point across. Why not? Because we are suffering from the Curse of Knowledge.

Once we know something, it is impossible to understand the situation from the perspective of someone who doesn't know it. We find it impossible to explain the product because we already know why it is so perfect. Stories can help us explain our products from the customer's perspective and avoid the Curse.

Stories define who we are and what we stand for

Stories are a way for you to tell your history, your values, and your vision without sounding like a braggart or being self-centered. You can tell your stories in a way that includes your listener so she can understand how she can be part of your story as well.

When you tell your vision story, your ideal customers will immediately become connected and will want you to succeed.

Stories build likability and trust

People buy from businesses they like and trust. Your stories, your customer stories, and your product stories can be the foundation of building that likability and trust. Stories enable you to get out of the features and benefits syndrome and get into engaging your reader.

Stories cannot be used for all marketing, all the time, and there is a place (and need) for identifying features and benefits But, when appropriate, stories can rivet your customers like no other marketing technique.

Stories humanize your business

If you have a business that is seen as official and impersonal, stories may be the way to personalize it. This doesn't mean that you should down play your expertise, stability, or security. It means that you can humanize the customer experience so the reader feels an attachment to how you deliver your expert services.

For example, a bank needs to explain its overdraft policies, but those policies will be full of legalize and appear coldhearted. A testimonial of a caring solution to a true customer experience can soften the required written policy.

Consider having your staff write stories. Get stories from your customers. Get involved with a local non-profit and tell their stories on your web site. Tell stories about your history. These stories often will include information about the community. You can be serious and human at the same time. Stories will help you do that.

Stories allow the reader to own the story

When a person reads a story she is creating mental images based on what she reads, but also using her own interpretations and related experiences. The story becomes her story. In a factual narrative, such as a product data sheet, the writer owns the content. It is much more effective to have your readers own the story than for them to just know your facts.

Stories are perfect for video

Humans are visual creatures and have been using images to communicate even before we had spoken language. We will be spending most of our time on writing stories. But anything written can be turned into a video, so be sure to consider video opportunities for your stories. Videos allow you to employ visual elements to support your brand personality and make the impact of the story even stronger.

Examples of Brands Using Stories

The easiest way to appreciate the power of story in marketing is to investigate some brands that do it well. You will notice that each of the following companies uses a different approach. For example, Three Twins Ice Cream uses mostly text-based stories and a very minimalist design. J. Peterman and Duluth Trading have well-developed visual elements that support their stories. The effect of their stories would be reduced without this visual reinforcement.

Note: Referencing web sites can be risky in a book, as brands have a way of changing their marketing, and examples used in a book can quickly become obsolete. However, here are a few that really seem to get story-based marketing, so perhaps they will keep it up!

J.Peterman

www.jpeterman.com

J. Peterman is one of the first and most memorable of the story-based brands. So famous it became part of the Seinfeld TV show, with character Elaine working for the iconic Mr. Peterman.

They do a great job of incorporating their story as well as stories of their partners, suppliers, and customers throughout their marketing. Pick any of their products and read the product description. Every one is a gem of a story woven with product features. They also offer a Quarterly Field Report they describe as "Travel is about story. Adventure. Heroes. Villains. Secrets. . ." Check out back issues to see if the Quarterly Field Report lives up to this enticing billing.

Sign up for their newsletter and note the playful way they advertise the current promotions. All are done with a nod to extending the story, both in words and in images.

Duluth Trading

www.duluthtrading.com

Duluth Trading is an online clothing retailer. Spend some time reading the product descriptions, looking at the images (illustrations rather than photographs), and see how their personality fits so well with the Duluth Lore and Timeline. They even include the story of the artist who illustrates their catalogues, as he is so integral to their look.

This is a clothing supplier for working men and women. No froufrou here. Just solid products with a "no bull guarantee." As with Saddleback Leather, they do a expert job of integrating the visual, the writing style, their archetype, and their story.

Saddleback Leather

www.saddlebackleather.com

Saddleback Leather has done a great job of supporting their story with dramatic visuals and overall design for a total experience based on their Explorer archetype (we will discuss archetypes in Chapter 4).

Review the images they use, the colors, the textures, the typography, and the overall feel of the site. Everything drives the Explorer message.

Saddleback Leather offers a 100-year guarantee, a pretty remarkable promise. But, their unexpected and bold tag line "They will fight over it when you are gone" stops you cold. With only nine words they have created a small story. You, as the customer, are the hero of this little story, but who are "they," and what happened to you? Saddleback Leather gives the reader the perfect opportunity to imagine a story that completely aligns with their brand archetype. Brilliant!

I dare you to read the story of the founder's dog, Blue, and not want to run out and buy a dog. You may not be their ideal customer, but you have to admire the great story-based brand they have developed.

Jessicurl

www.jessicurl.com

Jessicurl is a small business with a great founder's story. As a petite teen with very curly, flame red hair, Jessica was bullied for not "fitting in." The story of her quest to deal with her uncontrollable hair is alternately heart-breaking and laugh-out-loud funny.

Working in her kitchen she developed recipes for shampoo, conditioners, and other hair care products, which she started selling to fellow-curlies in a Yahoo Group.

From there it became a business, and as of this writing, she is selling products online and in stores in 17 countries.

More than just a seller of hair care products, Jessica is a role model for all teen girls who struggle with self-image issues. She has turned a personal challenge into a personal passion.

Take a look at her web site, videos, blog, and Facebook page for insight into what she does

NOTES

and how she uses stories to connect with people "suffering" with curly hair. Her motto is "You have the right to remain curly," and she lives that motto every day.

Three Twins Ice Cream

www.threetwins.com

Three Twins Ice Cream is a local favorite ice cream brand in Northern California. They promise "inconceivably delicious organic ice cream," and they really deliver on this promise. They take their ice cream very seriously—but not themselves. They also take their storytelling very seriously.

Visit the web site to see the founders' story, but also notice how stories are everywhere on this site: the story of each flavor, the story of their ingredients, the story of their flavors, even the story of their ice cream truck, Carl.

Of all the companies mentioned here, they may be the best example of building a story-based brand that is possible for the small business. A small business owner rarely has the resources for branding experts, expensive graphic designers, or professional writers. Three Twins Ice Cream is a more accessible model with a simple design and authentic stories that come from the heart.

The simplicity and sincere stories of Three Twins Ice Cream demonstrate a model any small business can work toward. You will have a different look and different stories. Your site may not be as creative, and your stories may need some polish, but you can craft stories like these around your business.

Spend some time on this site and identify where they have turned what could have been merely factual information into compelling stories.

NOTES

BASICS OF STORY WRITING

Four Critical Elements of a Story

Before we can begin to write our own stories, we must first understand what a story is. You may have never thought of defining story; most of us just "know a story when we hear it."

A story is a type of event-driven narrative that has four specific and necessary elements. Leave one of these elements out, and your story may just be a list of actions or an entertaining anecdote. It may be thought-provoking or funny, but it will not have the same impact on the reader as a true story.

Stories come in many types and levels of complexity from *Aesop's Fables* to Tolstoy's *War and Peace*. For our work, we will rely on the definition created by Kendal Haven, author of *Story Proof*. As he states in that book, this definition is fully supported by research, and "It is fully consistent with the documented activity of the mind."

Story: A detailed, character-based narration of a character's struggles to overcome obstacles and reach an important goal.

The Story Definition

A detailed	character-based narration
of a character's struggles to overcome obstacles	and reach an important goal

Story Definition Expanded

Let's look at each element of the story definition in a bit more detail.

A Detailed . . .

Details are the specifics that make your story real and memorable. They are usually sensory elements that help create the mental picture of your story.

Can you smell the lilacs growing in your spa courtyard? How does the leather of your messenger bag feel? What color sweater was your customer wearing? Can you describe the taste of your new ice cream? How cushy is your new chair? These details allow your story to connect with the reader through the shared sensory experiences.

Sometimes details may be important quantities. It holds 6 quarts, has 3 interlocking gears, or withstands winds of 100 mph. Details may be part of the conflict: it took 3 years to find a solution to her problem. You may think these sound a lot like features and benefits. You would be right if you just listed them in a bullet list. However, if you weave these into the telling of the story, they become memorable details. We can remember details when they are in a story, but not when they are in a list of unrelated items. Use this fact of the human brain to your advantage.

If you leave out important details, the reader will fill them in based on her own experiences. The reader's experiences may mean the story morphs into something unintended.

This phenomenon is at work when we read a book and then watch the movie, disappointed that the characters didn't look, sound, or behave as we expected. Due to your reader's life experiences, her version of your marketing story will always be unique, but you can make sure the story still conveys your message by including enough detail so your reader knows exactly what you mean.

Beware of burdening your story with unnecessary details, though. Stay focused on your message, or you may lose the reader's attention.

. . . character-based narration . . .

A story with no characters cannot exist. Think of a movie you have seen. Remove the characters and there is nothing left. You can have a great story with little physical action, as it may be

NOTES

_____

_____

_____

_____

_____

_____

_____

_____

_____

_____

_____

_____

_____

_____

_____

_____

_____

_____

_____

_____

_____

_____

_____

_____

_____

_____

_____

_____

NOTES

_____
_____
_____
_____
_____
_____
_____
_____
_____
_____
_____
_____
_____
_____
_____
_____
_____
_____
_____
_____
_____
_____
_____
_____
_____
_____
_____
_____
_____

an inner struggle, but you cannot have a story without characters.

In marketing stories, the listener may be one of the characters. You may be the central character in many of your stories, however, don't forget to include stories about your customers (or people who suffered because they were not customers), employees, partners, and others.

When using real people in your stories, you may make them anonymous. If you do use real names, or if the person can be readily identified, be sure to get permission.

... of a character's struggles to overcome obstacles ...

It is the struggle that makes the story so compelling. The drama of rising tension, the surprising twists, the suspense of "Will she make it?" are critical elements in a great story.

In marketing stories, the tension may be less obvious. Physical struggles or conflict between characters are not the only ways to include tension. The tension may be an internal struggle with objections. (Is it too expensive? Will it be easy to maintain? Will I really lose 10 pounds?) Tension can also be in the form of increasing features: "and you also get the second set of knives ... and the free dish towel ... and the sharpening stone."

... and reach an important goal.

If there is no goal, there is no reason to pay attention to the story. **In marketing, the goal focuses on what the listener needs** (look better, fix urgent problem, avoid machine downtime).

In marketing stories, these important goals are reached by others, and therefore, the listener feels she can achieve the goal as well.

Importance is in the mind of the listener. What is important to her, right now? What do you want her to do or think?

More than the Sum of its Parts

Just using the required elements of the story definition does not make a great story, any more than just mixing together random amounts of flour, milk, and eggs will give you a delicious cake.

But, by starting with these elements, we are on the path to writing a story. Our stories will describe the character and her struggles to reach an important goal. The plot (the events that make up the story) is derived from this struggle, and our included details will bring the character and the story to life.

Unlike entertaining stories, our marketing stories will also require a message.

Our goal is not to become entertainers (as some storytellers are) but to engage our ideal customers while imparting the information we want to communicate. A clear focus on our message will enable us to create the best stories—ones that stimulate the action we want the reader to take.

Preparation for the Story

With the generic definition of story behind us, we can now begin to work on a particular story. Read through the four steps that follow plus the Warm Up Exercise. This should get you ready to tackle your first written story.

Step 1 | Identify Your Situation

Marketing stories do not exist in a vacuum. First decide on why, where, and how this story will be used.

NOTES

NOTES

_____
_____
_____
_____
_____
_____
_____
_____
_____
_____
_____
_____
_____
_____
_____
_____
_____
_____
_____
_____
_____
_____
_____
_____
_____
_____
_____
_____

Why?

Why are you are telling this story? Can you state it in a short sentence? A phrase? A single word? A clear message will make the writing process so much easier and keep you focused on delivering that message.

A few examples are:
- What do you want the reader to do or think after reading it?
- What concept is the story teaching?
- What customer objection do you need to overcome?

Where?

Where will you be using this story:
- A networking event?
- A cold call?
- A sales call?
- On a web page?

Who?

Who is your reader?
- Your ideal customer?
- A general audience?
- What is her problem?
- What is her worldview? Worldview is discussed in Chapter 4.
- What about this person is important to the story?

How?
- Is this a written story or verbal?

Step 2 | Identify the four story elements

Characters

You may be in the story. The listener may be in the story. A previous customer, a staff member, or a competitor's customer may be in the story. Marketing stories tend to have only one or two characters. Leave out anyone who isn't absolutely essential to the story.

Goal

What is the goal your character is trying to reach? Why is this an important goal for her?

How can you describe the goal so it aligns with your reader's goal and fits with her experience?

Conflict

What trouble does your character have reaching this goal? Has she tried before and failed? Is the conflict recovery from a disaster? Is it an inner struggle or a physical struggle? Is it against another person, a force of nature, or just a situation?

Details

Which details will you need to include so your reader can identify with the story? Remember that to be effective the reader must be able to see herself in the story.

Deciding how much you need to explain about the characters, the situation, and the details of the struggle are all part of the art of writing, which you will be learning as you practice writing stories.

If details are missing or unfamiliar or too vague, the story will not have the desired effect; however, too many details may bog down the story.

NOTES

_____

_____

_____

_____

_____

_____

_____

_____

_____

_____

_____

_____

_____

The Story Arc

NOTES

_____

_____

_____

_____

_____

_____

_____

_____

_____

_____

_____

_____

_____

_____

_____

_____

_____

_____

_____

_____

_____

_____

_____

_____

_____

_____

_____

Step 3 | Review the story arc

Story arc is the trajectory of your story plot. The story arc is a useful tool when writing longer works, like novels and screenplays, but marketing stories are often so short that the story arc is compressed to only a paragraph or two. However, the concept that your story has a beginning (the introduction), something happens to change the status quo (the trigger), the conflict builds to a climax (another change of direction), and reaches resolution will probably be found, or implied, in most of your stories.

You may decide to leave out some of these plot features in the final story, or you may decide to rearrange the sequence of these events. However, it is a good training device to think about them before you start the actual writing. Without the underpinning of the story arc, you may find your story losing focus or direction.

Introduction
This is where your story starts. Whether everything is calm or in confusion, it is where we pick up the story. This can also be referred to as the exposition, as it is the background information necessary to understand the character and setting.

Trigger
The trigger is the event that upsets the status quo and changes the course of the story. This can be an internal change (a question, concern, or goal), or an external force (such as someone in trouble, an accident, or a friend needing help). Reacting to this trigger is what sets off the direction of the conflict.

Conflict
This is the driving force or tension of the story. It aligns with the human desire to avoid the unpleasant, so the conflict is the character's quest to return to harmony or avoid future problems. It may be a fevered physical battle or an internal struggle with the character's consciousness.

Climax

Climax is the point when the conflict is resolved. The dragon is slain, the lost son is found, the best mix of ingredients is found. The climax can also result in a change for the worse. Losing a key client results in business failure. A cheaper competitor's product is used, and all data is lost in a flood. Not all stories have happy endings, and that may be the message you wish to communicate.

Falling Action

The falling action is the returning to harmony, or to closure and acceptance. In marketing stories, this may be very brief.

Resolution

This is where we leave the story. The customer is happy, or in the case of her making a wrong decision, she realizes she should have chosen your product.

Warm Up Exercise

For your first writing exercise, it is often useful to tell a story you are not so close to. Start with this kite flying story. Feel free to be as wild as you like without worry about sticking to the facts given.

For this exercise, assume you are the owner of a kite store and want to explain why you founded this business and your passion for it.

Message

Kite flying is much more than a fun child's activity; it saved my family and it can save yours.

Characters

You (the owner) and a neighbor. You might decide to include one of your children.

Goal

To build a strong family bond through shared fun experiences.

Brand Brainstorming

Before you begin writing stories it is essential to think about how you will use them in your marketing.

Start now by thinking how stories fit into your brand personality. This is just your initial view—which may change as you begin using stories.

Possible uses for stories

_____

_____

_____

_____

_____

_____

_____

_____

_____

_____

_____

_____

_____

_____

_____

_____

Keep this list handy and update it as you go through this book.

Conflict

I had a dysfunctional family. My wife and I were busy working parents. Our children had their own activities (soccer, band, ballet). The kids were using their cell phones and game systems for entertainment and communication to such excess that we didn't talk much as a family. We had few common family activities; mostly we were busy getting each child to his/her own activities. We were not building any family memories.

Trigger

One day a neighbor made an observation about how scattered and stressed my family seemed.

Details

How much about my family do I want to include? How many children? Ages? Activities they are involved in? What did we do before that I found so enjoyable? What else can I say about my family so the reader will connect with my situation? How can I describe the kite store so people will understand why I am so passionate about it?

First draft

Using these elements, your story might start to look like this:

[intro] My family was like any other. Three kids and a dog living your average middle class life. The kids did well enough in school and had a boatload of extra curricular activities, like soccer, band, and ballet. I thought we were pretty much like other families.

[trigger] Then one day my neighbor made a comment about how my kids never acknowledged him any more. Every time he saw them, they were heads down with fingers tapping on their mobile devices. He said he missed the days when they were younger and friendlier.

[conflict] Wow. It never occurred to me that they weren't friendly. I started paying more attention and realized, sadly, that he was right.

I noticed they brought those devices to dinner and were always on them in the car. No more family conversation. No more family games to amuse us on road trips. We were turning into five people sharing a residence, almost like strangers in a boarding house, rather than a family.

I was determined to fix this situation and started looking for fun things we could do as a family. I needed something that would be challenging for the older ones and yet doable for my youngest.

[climax] That's when I stumbled into a kite store and realized it was the perfect family activity. The owner was retiring and was selling the store. Buying the kite store would fulfill a lifelong dream of owning my own business. It offered family-friendly hobbies and activities. I was able to help other families avoid the we-are-only-connected-via-our-technology-syndrome. Best of all, I got my family back!

What would your version of this story be?

Your First Story

Now is the time to start your first story. A good place to start is your passion story.

This is the story of what drove you to start your business. Developing a business is hard work, and without that inner passion, you would not be able to get up each day and keep at it.

What is your passion? Do you have an example that describes what inspired you to start this business rather than just getting a job? Or perhaps you experienced a situation that proved to you why your work is so fulfilling.

Remember that your story should have characters (probably you), details, a struggle to overcome obstacles, and an important goal.

If you need an example to get you going, check out the sample stories in Chapter 9. You can

NOTES

also read **My Story** below, which is my passion story.

My Story

You can thank Susan. She ignited my passion for using stories in marketing and for this book. For about a year I had been working with Susan on marketing her new home health care business. She had a great idea; one that was unique in our area. More importantly, it was a business that was rooted in her own painful experience with finding in-home care for her aging parents.

The web site was up and she was developing a name for herself in the local health care community. But progress was slow, and her branding really needed a boost.

Then she sent me an email. She had been featured in a local magazine. Her heart rending story of how she turned her life inside-out to care for her parents through failing health, Alzheimer's, surgeries, cross-country relocations, and home remodeling, all to give her parents the best care possible was there for the community to read.

I immediately called her to ask why this story was not on her web site. Why did I not know this story?

"I thought it was too personal. I didn't think others would care. I thought it didn't sound professional," came the hesitant reply.

I wanted to cry. Susan's story was exactly what her ideal customers needed to hear. They needed to know that she has walked the path they were now on. She had lived with the pain and the doubts and the heartache of watching a loved one suffer and finally die.

I have worked with many clients who have the same hesitancy in sharing their passion stories. But it was Susan's story that finally put me over the edge. I said, "No more!" I will not let clients get by with weak branding and wimpy web sites. I will not let them hide their passion. I will not let them miss great customer relationships because they don't understand their greatest asset is the story they have to tell.

I realized just talking to clients about the power of stories and recommending some great books on the subject were not enough. They needed to be shown the way to build a story-based brand and needed some nurturing in the process. That is when I decided to start offering workshops and to write this book.

Same Story Different Message

A single situation can provide many variations of a story, allowing you to tweak it for the situation and the message at hand.

To see how this works, let's take a look at a recent experience I had.

My knee began to bother me, and gradually the pain increased until I could no longer go up the stairs, walk for any distance, or move at a spced beyond a slow stroll. I work in an older two-story building, and my office is on the second floor. There is no elevator, so I need to get up those stairs.

My regular doctor suggested rest and pain medication. After 2 weeks the pain was still there, so off I went to the orthopedist. He felt it could be a bit more serious and gave me two options: X-Ray/MRI or physical therapy.

I decided to go both routes. We did an X-Ray (which did not reveal anything), and I signed up for physical therapy. The therapist did a few tests and observed me walk, do squats, etc. His diagnosis was my high arches threw my knees out of alignment when I walked. He suggested a regimen of exercises plus shoe orthotics to provide needed arch support.

NOTES

From One Comes Many

A good exercise for developing your story muscles is to take a single situation and see how many messages it can support.

Start by thinking of a situation with a customer. The situation needs to have the basics of a story: character (probably the customer), an important goal, details, and conflict. Perhaps it is a customer complaint that you successfully resolved. Or perhaps it is a happy customer calling with a testimonial that shows how your product or service overcame their initial objection. Maybe it is a story of a customer who bought a competitor's product first, was unhappy with it, and now bought yours. This is for practice so don't feel burdened to write a polished story.

What is the basic story plot?

Think of as many messages as you can where you can tweak this story to make it useful for one of your audiences.

Make a game out of it to see if you can keep coming up with more and more messages. It makes no difference if these messages are useful or not—or even realistic—the point of this exercise is to hone your ability to find multiple messages in a single situation.

I asked him about the need for an MRI. He was noncommittal, but added, "More information is always good." Meanwhile the orthopedist ordered the MRI that showed a possible slight tear in the meniscus. Worse, there were some suspicious dark areas on the thigh area—not related to this problem, but a concern.

The doctor felt it was probably nothing as I had no symptoms, but as the radiologist had suggested a bone scan of these mysterious spots, he was obliged to order that test as well.

So I went through the process of the injection with the radioactive solution, worrying about what they would find, and the scan itself. Turns out it was nothing. Meanwhile my knee felt better, and I was back to my normal activities.

I met once again with the orthopedist, and we decided that as I was not feeling any more pain and could do my normal activities, I should continue on with the exercises and orthotics and see how it goes.

$5000 for unnecessary tests, but I was walking again!

How could I use this story? I could use portions of it to illustrate any of the following messages:

- **More information is not necessarily a good thing.** By going for the MRI, I opened the door to other unrelated issues that required time, worry, risk, and money only to find they were unnecessary. (Note the bone scan was unnecessary in my case, but this does not mean all extra tests should be avoided.)
- **The most obvious answer (knee problems) might not be the right one.** Are you focusing on the symptom (knee pain) and mistaking it for the problem? Or should you look further for the real culprit (the arches)?
- **The value of a second opinion.** Having both opinions gave me the knowledge that 1) yes, there is a small meniscus tear which might resolve itself or develop into

something that needs surgery down the road, and 2) I have an arch problem that needs addressing before it causes serious, permanent problems.

- **Starting with the least invasive remedy may be the best approach.** The least invasive route is usually less risky and less costly. It also leaves the door open for other more invasive procedures should they be needed. All it really takes is a bit of patience to work through the options from least to most invasive.

- **A specialist looking at your problem will find one that she is able to fix.** This is true in all fields. Ask an SEO practitioner about your web site, and she will find all sorts of "problems" she can fix for you. Ask a social media specialist, and she will assure your lack of business is only an improved Facebook page away (and she, of course, can make this happen).

By adjusting the details of the story to the message, I can use this same experience for multiple purposes. I can keep the story with all the details or delete those that aren't necessary to the message I want.

By the way, note the story arc at work here:

[intro] I was physically fine, then one day I started noticing pain.

[trigger] One day I could not go up the stairs.

[rising conflict] I started visiting doctors and a therapist looking for a solution. Physical exams, tests, X-Ray, MRI, bone scan, exercise, shoe orthotics, etc. Physical therapy. Lots of money being spent, still in pain and being inconvenienced by all this.

[climax] Suddenly the pain stopped.

[falling action] Was it the therapy? The shoe orthotics? The tear healing itself? I don't know. But more tests won't give me the answer.

Need Inspiration?

If you are still in need of ideas or samples of stories to get you started, get some back issues of *Inc.* magazine.

Almost every article in the magazine will begin with a story.

Each month's issue has a theme and some great one-page stories. This month it is "How I Got Started." The stories cover how eight well-known and respected entrepreneurs got their starts. You can be sure that any story of an entrepreneur has plenty of challenges, conflicts, and plot twists. There is always a message.

Go through a few of these to analyze each article. Who are the characters? Can you spot the story arc points? What is the climax? What is the message?

Were any points left out? Did it make a difference to you?

How much of the story are you filling in yourself?

They have excellent writers. Analyzing great writing is a potent tool to improve your own writing skills. As William Zinsser, author of *On Writing Well,* so perfectly states, "Writing is learned by imitation. We all need models."

Aspiring jazz musicians hang out at clubs to hear the masters perform, rookie baseball players watch videos of future Hall of Famers play. Take your cue from these high achievers and learn from experienced writers.

NOTES

[resolution] I have a greater awareness of my arch situation and how to deal with it. I am walking (and climbing stairs) just fine.

Note that not all of these stages in the story arc need to be present in every version of the story. In fact, including them all would be tedious and ruin the drama. Only use the story arc elements you need to support your message and keep your story interesting.

Stuck for Story Ideas?

You may be thinking that you have no story ideas, or perhaps you have one idea but feel that is all you will ever have. There are usually two factors in play here:

- You haven't really thought much about telling stories until now.
- You are looking for the "really big story" and missing so many opportunities.

The stories you need for your business are not *Harry Potter* or *Star Wars* epics. We love these big stories because they take us out of our daily routine and into a fantasy. They are an escape from our problems.

As a business owner, you are offering a solution to at least one of your ideal customers' every day problems. You are not offering an escape from a problem; you are offering to fix it.

When you focus on trying to find a big story, you miss all the wonderful small stories that will engage your ideal customer. It isn't the size of your story that is important, it is the relevance and how you tell it.

Think of a rough gem that is laying on the ground. Most people wouldn't even notice it. But eventually one person sees the glint, picks it up, and sees the potential. With a little cleaning, shaping, and polishing, it is starting to look good. Placed in attractive setting and worn with a complementary outfit, it has become something remarkable.

Your stories will be like those overlooked rough stones. Your must find these hidden gems and shape them by providing context and meaning.

Take a look at the John Jantsch positioning story in Chapter 9. This is a simple story and yet very powerful. From it we know exactly the kind of clients Jantsch likes to work with.

In order to create your own stories from everyday events, try using the three-way viewing technique described below.

Three-way viewing

Start with any small event that you can think of. Don't worry if you don't have a message or characters or conflict or any of the other story requirements. Got an event in mind? Now think about the:

- **Details.** Describe the event in detail. What exactly happened? Who was there? What were the expressions on their faces? What might have they been thinking? Was there any physical action? Were there any physical objects involved?
- **Backstory.** What happened leading up to this event? This might be a long simmering issue or a sudden comment.
- **Future.** What happened after the event? What were the implications? Did it change anyone? Did it change anything about your business?

Example

Let's try the three-way view with a simple example of a customer returning a product. On the surface this is a routine event for anyone selling products. In fact, it is probably so routine you don't even think about it anymore. And, like that rough stone in the dirt, you may be missing the gems.

- **Details.** Describe the event and every detail you can remember. Who was present? Was it a new employee? A loyal customer? Were other customers watching? Why was the customer unhappy with the product? What was her tone

Three-Way Viewing

Think of something that happened today. How can you turn this routine event into a story? First identify the event and then apply the three-way view.

Event

Details

Backstory

Future

NOTES

_____

_____

_____

_____

_____

_____

_____

_____

_____

_____

_____

_____

_____

_____

_____

_____

_____

_____

_____

_____

_____

_____

_____

_____

_____

_____

of voice? Was the employee defensive? Confident? Did the employee process the return appropriately? Was the customer satisfied? Was she likely to buy from you again or frustrated with the experience?

♦ **Backstory.** What led up to this event and the characters reactions? Are you having trouble with this product? Are your employees fully trained on customer service policies? Are your policies too restrictive and thus annoy your customers? Are you more concerned about losing a sale than keeping the customer happy? Do you have a return policy, but no story like Nordstrom that gives your employees the freedom to act as you would like? Does a return demonstrate that the customer was sold an unsuitable product in the first place?

♦ **Future.** What was the result? Could it have been a better experience for the customer? Does this indicate you should improve your sales training program? Or you should improve your employee's customer service skills? Is your marketing setting you up to attract the wrong customers or creating wrong expectations? Perhaps the customer left happy at the ease of the process, and you realized that everything was working just as you had hoped!

Somewhere in almost every situation we face as a business owner is a story. Depending on the details, this routine sales event could be used in an employee meeting to congratulate a new employee on demonstrating great service. Or it could be used on your web site to demonstrate how you treat your customers. Perhaps the customer in the story would give a testimonial.

Perhaps, while reviewing the customer who left angry about not being able to make a product return, you realized you are too focused on the sales numbers and are really hurting your business by driving loyal customers away. Was this was a turning point in your approach to customer service?

What about this story will now connect with your ideal customer? Or perhaps it will inspire an employee. Or maybe it isn't a useful story at all! Not all rocks will become beautiful no matter how much you polish them. However, the exercise of analyzing events will pay off when you become proficient in seeing the story possibilities in everyday events.

Before Moving On

Are you now starting to recognize a true story when you hear it? Are you getting comfortable with writing basic stories? Are you starting to see story opportunities all around you? Keep developing these skills as you move on to the next chapter.

Extra Credit

How is your first story going? Let it sit for a bit and then go back and re-read it. Sometimes you need a break to see your work with fresh eyes.

What can you do to improve it? One method that may improve it is to rearrange the sequence of events. In the kite store example, the first draft is in strict chronological sequence and follows the story arc. But sometimes that produces a very predictable and boring story line.

Take a cue from screen writers and novelists and try a different approach. Start at the end of the story and then "flash back" to earlier events.

In the kite story, I could start with the result, such as, "Who would have guessed that a smart-phone could change my life?" Then I would go back to recap how I made this life changing and family-changing journey. Can you rearrange your story elements for greater drama?

If you are not satisfied with your story, don't worry. We will learn how to improve your stories in Chapter 6. For now, just keep writing.

NOTES

YOUR IDEAL CUSTOMER

Reaching Your Ideal Customer

Trying to reach everyone is a waste of time and the road to business failure. No business is ideal for everyone. Not Walmart. Not Target. Not Apple. But each has a clearly defined ideal customer.

Clearly identifying your ideal customer (or customers) is the crucial first step to successful marketing. So how do you identify your ideal customer?

Traditionally, marketers used the terms target audience or target market. These were often based on demographics (statistical characteristics of a population, such as age, gender, education, income, or geographic location, etc.) plus some indiction of their psychographics. Psychographics are more than who these people are. Psychographics are the values, motivations, lifestyles, and behaviors that influence their decisions.

Psychographic values might be level of self-esteem, price sensitivity, technology adoption, personal archetype, etc. Understanding your ideal customers' psychographics is important, as the more you can "get inside the head" of your ideal customer, the greater your chance of fulfilling their desires.

Target audience is such an impersonal label. That is why thinking in terms of ideal customer is more useful. It helps you think about an individual, one who you can really discover and talk to.

The easiest way to identify an ideal customer (including both demographic and psychographic attributes) is to think of your best customers. Best customers may be those who buy the most from you, or better yet, those who seem to really love what you offer and refer their friends to you.

The attraction of insects to flower attributes is an especially fitting analogy for your ideal customers' attraction to your business.

Another way to look at this is to think, "If I could have 100 customers like Joan, I would be happy and successful."

So who is "Joan"? What are her demographic and psychographic attributes?

If you don't have existing customers (or sadly, don't have the right customers) you have to spend more time thinking about, and perhaps researching, whom you want to attract.

Use the Exercise Box to the right to start documenting attributes of your ideal customer. You will probably have more than one ideal customer. You may also have subsets of a primary ideal customer.

For example, if you own a yarn shop, you may have beginning knitters as well as very experienced knitters. You may have senior women who make afghans for the homeless shelter and teenage girls who want to create their own unique fashion accessories.

At first glance this may seem like four primary ideal customer categories (beginners, experienced knitters, seniors, teen girls). But you may find that teenage girls have more in common with each other (sense of fashion, need to be seen as trendy, reliance on technology for information and social connections), regardless of skill, than they do with senior women. After reflection, you may decide that you have two main ideal customers: senior women and teenage girls. Within each of those primary categories you will have beginners and experienced knitters as subcategories.

As your business grows, you may start to identify new ideal customer categories. However, be careful about having too many categories, especially too many primary categories. The goal of identifying your ideal customers is to create products, services, and marketing efforts that satisfy the desires of each. Too many categories will have you going crazy with too many options. It is better to have

Your Ideal Customer

Name of ideal customer
Give your ideal customer a name, even if it is a fictitious customer.

List all relevant demographics

Why is she an ideal customer?

What values does she have that will attract her to your business?

What behaviors does she exhibit?
Where does she shop? What are her routine activities, online usage, social activities, etc.?

What groups does she belong to?
List social, business, religious, political or educational possibilities.

What causes does she support?

What are her priorities in life?

How would she describe her lifestyle?

What are her fears or worries?
Once you have answered all these questions (and any others you think are relevant) create a profile of this person—a narrative that creates a real, breathing, ideal customer description.

fewer ideal customer categories with robust and clearly differentiated programs for each.

Resonance or Pollination?

Now that you have identified your ideal customers, you know what will resonate with them.

Resonance is a phenomenon of physics where systems have a tendency to vibrate at specific frequencies. Resonance is also a marketing concept: we want our offerings to resonate with our customers. Resonance, however, is one dimensional. I believe a stronger, multidimensional analogy comes from the world of insects, flowers, and pollination.

Flowering plants are not able to reproduce by themselves. They need the help of various insects and birds to spread their pollen. To woo these creatures, flowers have developed sophisticated attraction mechanisms: a floral branding campaign!

The direct parallels between flower pollination and business marketing are astounding.

Just as our businesses will wither if no one buys, if no insect visits the flower and carries away the pollen, the plant is not able to fulfill its mission of reproducing.

Over the millennia, flowers have created an astonishing variety or characteristics. Some have evolved to appeal to the masses. They are brightly colored and grow in large groupings to be visible from the ground or the air. These mass market flowers make it easy for almost any insect, no matter how inept, to get their nectar and be covered in pollen.

Other plants are more selective and have evolved to appeal to a narrow type of insect, one that is able to navigate its intricate structure. Ah—mass appeal vs. ideal customer!

This partnership works when the flowers have invested in creating the right attraction elements, and the insects are present to be receptive to these elements and spread the pollen.

Flowers are not limited to just shape, color, and scent, which are the elements we most frequently notice and care about. Flowers also have specific temperatures. Bees use energy to stay warm and so look for warm flowers. They can then get the nectar and a bit of warmth to conserve their own energy.

Recently scientists have found that an electric field is another tool for flowers to attract insects. Flowers have a slight negative charge. Bees also have an electric charge. The friction between their body parts and the air as they are flying makes the bees positively charged, and when they land on a flower, the negatively charged pollen naturally sticks to it. What is even more interesting is that this change in the plants natural electric charge remains for about 100 seconds. This is an indicator to other insects flying by that the flower has been visited. It is basically a "sold out" sign on the flower.

When you are defining your ideal customer, think like a flower. Whom do you want to attract? What are they looking for? What will make it easier to buy from you? What will make your flower stand out in the crowded field?

So often when a marketing campaign fails, the marketers complain that people didn't "get it" as if it is the customers' fault.

The customer is not at fault; the marketing message was not sending the right signals.

The key concept here is that you need to adjust your marketing to send those signals that are attractive to your ideal customer. How do you know the right signals? By a thorough understanding of what motivates your ideal customers.

Without this all of your marketing will be hit or miss.

NOTES

NOTES

WorldView

Worldview is a psychographic element you can use to test and refine your ideal customer profile.

Worldview is a term popularized by Seth Godin, author of *All Marketers Are Liars*. In that book he defines worldview as the "rules, values, beliefs, and biases that an individual customer brings to a situation."

We see the impact of individual worldviews everyday in the news, especially in the political arena. In the United States, we have views on immigration policy that range from pro-immigration folks who see immigrants as a continuation of their own history. Their view is we are a nation of immigrants, and we would not be successful as a nation without continued welcoming of new immigrants.

Those on the opposite side of the discussion see new immigrants as burdening our social services while they are taking jobs from existing citizens. There are, of course, many views in between these extremes.

This issue is hard to resolve as the opinions are based on worldview more than facts. It is extremely difficult to get someone to change her worldview based on a debate of the issues alone.

Some other worldviews are:
- I must do my part to protect the planet vs. The problems are too big for my little contribution to help, so why bother?
- Most people are not trustworthy, so I am always expecting someone to take advantage of me vs. Most people are really trying to do the right thing, so I give them the benefit of the doubt.
- Your appearance is important in making a good impression, and I feel better about myself when I am dressed appropriately vs. My appearance reflects who I am and I don't care what you think. I dress to please myself.

- I am very health conscious and only eat organically produced foods that are grown locally vs. I buy based on price and convenience. The health nuts are just trying to scare us.
- Dogs are more dependable than people, and I spend a lot of money on keeping my dog happy vs. Dogs are expensive and messy. People spend to much money on pets. They are just animals, and there are so many other worthy causes.

Worldviews are be shaped by our family, friends, and by our experiences. If your family always had dogs, you may have learned responsible behavior by caring for them. You may have also learned to be considerate of animals and to enjoy the companionship of a dog. If you never were allowed a pet as a child, you might not have the same appreciation for dogs, and may find people foolish for spending lavishly on their pets.

Our worldviews are what enable two people to view the same situation or set of facts and come up with completely different decisions. We all have our worldviews, and we all believe our worldviews are right.

You cannot change someone's worldview. Facts, features, and benefits will not get her to budge.

Instead, embrace your shared worldview to let it attract your ideal customers.

Worldview Example

To see worldview in action, pretend your market research shows that your new product will appeal to early boomer men who are married with adult children, very wealthy, well known in their field, eat little or no meat, are Monty Python fans, either British or have an affinity for things British, and buy the best (since they can afford it).

Does this sound like a complete picture of an ideal customer?

Worldviews

Test your worldview ideas on the five web sites you reviewed earlier:
- www.jpeterman.com
- www.duluthtrading.com
- www.saddlebackleather.com
- www.jessicurl.com
- www.threetwinsicecream.com

Answer the following questions about each one:

What is the worldview of this business?

What is the worldview of its ideal customers?

What elements on the site tell you about their worldview?
- Logo?
- Tag line?
- Colors?
- Layout?
- Tone of voice?
- Examples?
- Imagery?
- *About Us* page?
- Product mix?
- Testimonials?
- Return Policy?
- Newsletter?

Now review your own web site. What does it say about your worldview? If it isn't in alignment with the worldview of your ideal customers, what can you do to fix it?

NOTES

_____
_____
_____
_____
_____
_____
_____
_____
_____
_____
_____
_____
_____
_____
_____
_____
_____
_____
_____
_____
_____
_____
_____
_____
_____
_____
_____
_____
_____

What if you learned that both Ozzy Osborne and Prince Charles fit this picture? Now do you think it is a complete picture?

Both Prince Charles and Ozzy were born in England in 1948. Both are fabulously wealthy and international celebrities. They both are on their second marriages and have adult children. Ozzy is a vegetarian and Prince Charles is an avid environmentalist who eats little meat.

But that isn't the whole picture.

Prince Charles' worldview is one of tradition, stability, and legacy. He has lived his whole life by the rules and traditions of the monarchy. He is concerned about the environment and protecting the planet for future generations, and will become the Defender of the Faith when he becomes King.

Ozzy, on the other hand, grew up in poverty, failed at school, and found his own way to success. His worldview is one of making his own way, never living within convention, seeking the outrageous, and opposing organized religion.

So what does this mean to you as a marketer? Make sure your ideal customer descriptions and their worldviews are as complete as possible. More importantly, their worldviews that influence their buying of your products must be your worldview.

In other worlds, don't bother selling Ozzy a Saville Row suit or giving Prince Charles a gift certificate to your tattoo parlor.

NOTES

ARCHETYPES

As we work through this chapter, it is good to remind ourselves of the big picture. Effective marketing requires the company understand its archetype, build its business around this understanding, and use its archetype to craft stories that resonate with its ideal customers.

What Are Archetypes?

Superman. The Prodigal Son. Romeo and Juliet. Pinocchio. Icarus. Sampson. These are stories of characters that transcend time, place, culture, gender, and age. They represent eternal truths. They are archetypes.

If you have seen *Star Wars* you understand the Hero and his journey through Luke Skywalker. In *The Karate Kid*, Mr. Miyagi is the classic Sage. Robin Williams in *Mrs. Doubtfire* is a Caregiver with a surprising twist.

People have archetypes. Your sister may be the Caregiver in the family. She is the one everyone seeks for help through troubled times. Perhaps your brother is the Sage. He is the one who always knows how to fix your computer, which TV model to buy, or helps you think through important decisions. You may have another brother who just never quite fit in. You could count on him to be the Rebel, finding his own way and marching to his own drummer. When you hosted a formal party, he showed up in a rumpled Grateful Dead T-shirt.

Companies have archetypes as well, and manifesting your company archetype enables you to signal your qualities to your ideal customers. Flowers send distinct signals of shape, color, fragrance, temperature, and electric field. Your brand archetype will send signals through colors, images, writing tone, products and services offered, naming conventions, and more to the marketplace. Just as the bees find the right flower for nectar, your ideal customers will find you.

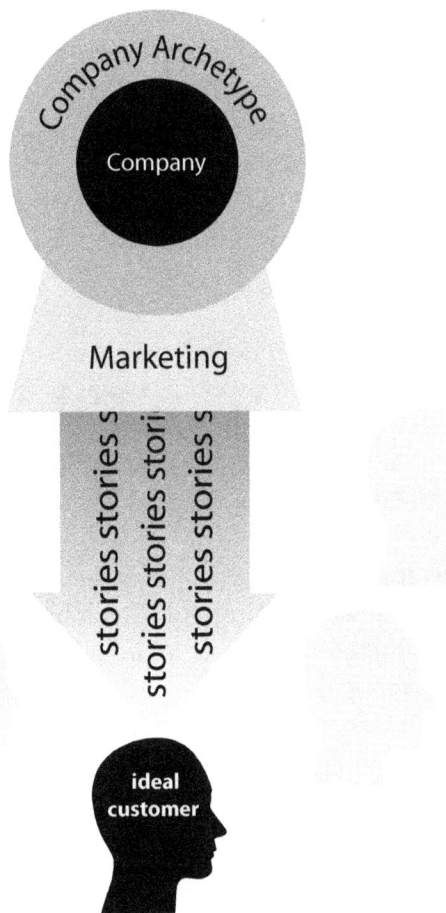

Why Are Archetypes Important?

Nurturing your company archetype is one secret to attracting your ideal customer.

Your archetype will help define your language and your visual elements—soft pastels and comforting images for a Caregiver, action shots and strong contrasts for an Explorer.

The kinds of images you need to use, both verbal and visual, become obvious. However, don't overlook your product names, tag line, packaging, business locations, partners, customer service policies, and all the other places you touch a costumer. All of these should flow from your archetype.

Your archetype is not your customer's
We are talking about **your company archetype** as we go through this chapter. Customers will probably have different personal archetypes.

For example, customers may want a Caregiver brand for their day care service, a Sage brand when they need to make difficult choices that require research, and a Jester brand when they feel like getting out of their normal routine and doing something outrageous. Customers may thus be attracted to many archetypes depending on their mood, the product, or the situation.

There are situations where your archetype is the same as your customer's. The Creator archetype may be yours as well as your customer's. **As you read through the archetypes, remember that we are talking about defining your archetype.**

As a company, you need to understand your core archetype and then use it to create your company personality. You will be staying true to this archetype, both internally and externally.

It is this resolute expression of your archetype that will attract your ideal customers. Know yourself, know your ideal customers, identify your archetype, and write stories that create an Unstoppable Brand.

Archetypes, Not Straightjackets

The following descriptions are summaries of 12 major archetypes that are appropriate for company branding.

Each of these 12 can be considered a fundamental archetype that describes a family of related archetypes. Use the descriptions that follow as an introduction to archetypes and for general insights into each of the 12 archetypes.

Successful businesses embrace their archetypes. Harley Davidson is clearly a Rebel. Other businesses, especially startups, may not have thought about an archetype. This can lead to disjointed marketing efforts and a confused message to the marketplace. If your web site reflects a Ruler archetype but your workshops project a Jester, your customers will be confused. Confused people do not buy.

If you find an archetype that is close but not quite a perfect fit, you may want to explore other resources that go into variations on these archetypes and introduce the other "family members." See Chapter 10 for these additional resources.

Beware of being too much of a slave to your archetype. Don't think of the archetype as a straightjacket. Instead, use your archetype to help you stay true to your authentic self while you can develop your own flavor. Star Trek and Amazon may share the Explorer archetype, but each has its own way of expressing it.

The 12 Main Archetypes

The 12 archetypes we discuss can be placed into four general families:

Structure Providers
These are archetypes that maintain order and protect others. They all seek to provide environments that are stable and predictable.

1. **Caregiver** who sacrifices herself to help others
2. **Creator** who uses her creativity to create order out of a chaotic world
3. **Ruler** who uses her power to make the world orderly

Paradise Seekers

These are the brands seeking a return to the "good old days" and simpler times, whether or not there ever were these good and simple days. They may seek to avoid materiality in our consumer-driven world and yearn for a more spiritual existence, whether that is within the person or in the world at large.

4. **Innocent** who seeks to return to the good old days
5. **Explorer** who seeks to find her paradise through exploration
6. **Sage** who seeks truth and knowledge of a better life

Everyman

These brands are the Average Guys who fulfill our need to connect with other humans and belong. This group helps us fit in and feel good about ourselves and the world.

7. **Regular Guy** who just wants to fit in
8. **Lover** who wants to be attractive and surrounded by sensuous things
9. **Jester** who shows us how to have fun

Change Agents

These archetypes use their special powers, whether the physical power of the Hero or the supernatural power of the Magician. They are able to change their reality and ours. Regardless of skills, they are about change—good or bad.

10. **Hero** who is willing to suffer to champion the underdog
11. **Rebel** who is willing to create revolution to make change
12. **Magician** who makes change through transformation

Structure Providers

Caregiver

Nurses, Mother Theresa, Florence Nightingale, Princess Diana, the country doctor, the neighborhood cop, and Mr. Rogers are all Caregivers.

The movie *It's a Wonderful Life* is a classic caregiver story, and George Bailey serves as a role model for all caregivers, sacrificing his own desires for travel and adventure to serve others in his town and continue his father's values.

The Caregiver is compassionate, generous, and nurturing, and above all an altruist. Caregivers are moved by a desire to help others avoid pain and uncertainty. They are powerful maternal figures, but not all caregivers are female. They fear instability, uncertainty, and chaos.

Some brands, such as insurance companies, telephone providers (AT&T), hospitals, and banks would naturally fit in this category. Unfortunately, it is all too easy for a for-profit organization to focus on the profits and betray their Caregiver archetype. This is a serious flaw and undermines the authenticity of the brand archetype. We all have our own horror stories of insurance claims denied, exorbitant phone bills, excessive bank fees, or denied loans, and have developed a thick skepticism when companies in these industries pretend to be Caregivers.

When marketing as a Caregiver, you must demonstrate how you truly care about your customers. Hollow platitudes about great customer service are not sufficient; you will need to prove it. However, spectacular customer service can really payoff for this archetype, as we see with Nordstrom. This is a natural archetype for home health agencies, visiting nurses, non-profits, and other nurturing brands.

Caregiver Brands
Mother Nature, Allstate Insurance, Dove, Volvo, Amnesty International, Sesame Street, OXO, and Campbell's Soup.

Creator

Frank Loyd Wright, Sir Richard Branson, Lego, Martha Graham, and Thomas Edison are examples of Creators. Creators long to create something of enduring value, have a passionate need for self-expression, and/or need to be cultural pioneers.

They are in the Structure group of archetypes because their work is a means to control their world.

Artists, innovators, entrepreneurs, chefs, musicians, and inventors fall in this category. Self-expression is their passion, and their creations give them a form of immortality, whether it be the Eiffel Tower or a new vacuum cleaner.

Brands in this archetype tend to be non-conformist but are quite different than the Rebel, as they are about creation rather than destruction.

This archetype appeals to the do-it-yourselfer. This means the Creator archetype will work for creative customers with considerable disposable income, the tech-savvy person venturing into the new 3D printer world, as well as the frugal home crafter.

The Creator archetype is a good fit for marketers, designers, public relations firms, arts organizations, and all tech innovation companies. It is also a good fit for companies with products that encourage self-expression in their customers, such as Crayola and hobby stores.

Creators must be aware of the possible trap of perfectionism. Martha Stewart is a Creator who attracts people who like her style and are able to handle perfectionism. But others are put off by this. Fortunately, there is room for all positions on the creative spectrum.

Giving your customers choices in your products will appeal to this group. Helping people avoid the mediocre will also be appealing. Thus Apple's iPhoto, which allows even the design-challenged to create stunning photo books, is a good example of the Creator in action.

Creator Brands
Crayola, LEGO, IDEO, Etsy, Adobe, Pinterest, Children's Television Productions, and 3M.

Ruler

The IRS, Brooks Brothers, Day-Timers, traditional banks, IBM, and Rolls Royce are familiar Ruler brands. They set the rules that the rest of their industry must follow.

The core desires of the Ruler brand is to control and exert leadership. They live by "power isn't everything, it's the only thing."

Being a Ruler isn't necessarily negative. A ruler provides structure to avoid chaos. Rulers are able to successfully drive a vision (think Steve Jobs at Apple). They are brand category leaders to whom the other brands must play catchup, that is until another brand does something revolutionary and leapfrogs the brand leader. Rulers run the risk of being bossy and authoritarian, and may limit innovation.

It is difficult to maintain a Ruler archetype as a brand these days. Absolute rulers are gone from the political scene, except for in a few fringe countries. Customers do not want to be your "serfs." It is no longer possible to operate in isolation; you must depend on employees and partners and even the social media universe. The old days of the invulnerable industry leader are over. New technology, social media, and crowd-based thinking have seen to that.

However, it is still possible to be the industry standard and provide stability to your customers. Just don't abandon innovation and always be sensitive to your customer's feelings. These days we all want to be Rulers!

The Ruler archetype works well for companies that help make people more organized, offer a life time guarantee, empower people to get control, have a protective function, and are the industry standard. Day-Timers is a brand that fits this definition.

Ruler Brands

IBM, Rolls Royce, Barclays Bank, and Microsoft.

Paradise Seekers

Innocent

Pollyanna, Forrest Gump, and Scout in *To Kill a Mockingbird* are all examples of the Innocent in action. This archetype believes there was a golden age when all was perfect and is seeking to return there.

Today those in this archetypes align with the Back to Basics movement and environmental causes. They espouse fundamental values, purity, and common sense. The Innocent is also the eternal optimist. Her core desire is to experience paradise (as she defines it), and her goal is to be happy.

If your brand archetype is the Innocent, you offer your ideal customers faith and optimism. Innovation is not a strong characteristic for this archetype; predictability is more often seen.

This archetype is frequently used for children's products, as well as for senior products and services. At these times in life people are able to focus on the simple life without the distractions of jobs, children, and financial worries.

In marketing to Innocents, you need to fulfill their need for certainty, offer positive and hopeful ideas, and demonstrate good moral choices. The promise of rescue and redemption also falls in this archetype.

Beware: the Innocent is very trusting. Never betray her. If your brand is an Innocent, you must be absolutely true and respectful of your customers' values. This is where Kashi went wrong in promoting its healthy grains while using GMO soybeans. (Read more about the Kashi issue in Chapter 7.)

Innocent Brands
Real Simple magazine, Coke, Disney, Pillsbury Doughboy, Ivory soap, Method household cleaning products, and Amy's Kitchen.

Explorer

Explorers crave new experiences, love to travel, and seek independence. They are individualistic and see themselves as outsiders to the rest of the world. Their motto is "Don't fence me in."

They want the freedom to discover themselves and lead a more authentic and fulfilling life.

In marketing to Explorers you need to value change more than consistency, let your customers express their individuality through your brand, and adapt to their restless spirits.

People attracted to this archetype in a brand do not want the hard sell. They much prefer to find you, rather than be targeted by your advertising. Viral marketing is more valuable than AdWords for this group.

The Explorer archetype is often especially appealing to youth and those recapturing youth. These are people who are marching to a different drummer, at least at this point in their lives.

Loyalty from this group can be difficult as they are always seeking something new. In order to retain customer loyalty you need to be totally authentic and address your customers' needs for new experiences.

People seeking the Explorer brand may not be obvious. Think of the buttoned-down accountant who plays in a rock band on the weekend or is planning a white water rafting vacation. This hidden aspect to their personalities is a surprise twist that can be utilized by some Explorer brands.

Explorer Brands
The Star Trek series, Patagonia outdoor wear, Jeep Wrangler, Starbucks, Amazon, General Food International Coffees, and Saddleback Leather.

Sage

Confucius, Marie Curie, Yoda, Oprah, Walter Cronkite, Socrates, Betty Crocker, and Galileo are all Sages. Sages desire truth and knowledge.

Sages believe in the human capacity to learn and grow, so it is a fitting archetype for educational organizations, as well as brands offering advice, information, and/or guidance. Sage brands are thoughtful and independent.

When marketing as a Sage, credibility is crucial. People attracted to this archetype want information, but they also want to think for themselves. They want information supported by data and won't accept a hard sell or someone talking down to them. They want to feel like experts themselves.

A trap for Sage customers is paralysis by analysis: the need to study issues and keep seeking more information but never acting. A Sage brand needs to provide value in the form of information (Google, NPR, CNN), but also in a way that allows their customers to make decisions and act (Consumer Reports, Mayo Clinic).

Sage brands must never use their knowledge unwisely or dupe their customers. Ideal customers for Sage brands will appreciate marketing that makes them think. These customers will do considerable research before buying, either on the web or in stores. They enjoy the research process. Sage marketing is often dignified, subtle, and possibly elitist. This allows Sage brands to enjoy a higher price point (Harvard University is able to charge more than the local state college). Expert endorsements are a plus; celebrity endorsements will not be. A successful strategy is to have known experts in the field use your products.

Sage Brands
National Public Radio, Harvard University, Mayo Clinic, The Smithsonian, Google, Consumer Reports, and The Teaching Company.

Everyman

Regular Guy

Situation comedies like *Everybody Likes Raymond*, County and Western music, blue jeans, and Homer Simpson are all in the Regular Guy archetype. The Regular Guys show us the virtues of being an ordinary person. Their motto is, "What you see is what you get." They desire to connect with others and to belong, to fit in. They have a common touch and display ordinary virtues. They offer us empathy and lack of pretense. They are not interested in being the hero or being in the spotlight. They do not crave excitement or adventure.

Brands in this archetype have great strength, faithfulness, usefulness, and resourcefulness. They have a common touch and offer realism, empathy, and lack of pretense.

People attracted to Regular Guy archetypes are put off by artifice or hype. They are drawn to down home, no nonsense brands. One useful attribute of the Regular Guy is the interest in belonging. If they connect with your brand and care about it, you can develop very loyal customers. Regular Guy brands can create tribes for long-term success.

In marketing, the casual approach may work the best; be understated, nonthreatening, and helpful.

Regular Guy Brands

Wendy's, Jimmy Dean Sausage, Duluth Trading Company, Geico Insurance, Kickstarter, Craig's List, and Trader Joe's.

Lover

Beauty and the Beast, Romeo and Juliet, Ingrid Bergman, Humphrey Bogart, Guinever and Lancelot, and Marilyn Monroe all fit in the Lover archetype. Lover brands are not just the obvious sexually-oriented brands like Victoria's Secret. Godiva and Häagen-Dazs are also lover brands. The Lover archetype is about intimacy and experience, but also attractiveness and living through the senses.

Lovers exhibit great passion and appreciation of beauty. Lover brands will need carefully developed visual elements that support an appropriate sensuousness.

People attracted to Lover brands are looking for deeper connections, even with companies and products. They are seeking companies with intimate and elegant cultures. They expect beauty and quality in all aspects of the brand and appreciate subtly. They are also willing to pay for this differentiation.

Blatantly attracting attention and shallowness should be avoided.

Lover brands are common in the cosmetics, jewelry, fashion, travel, and high-end food and wine industries. If your brand promises beauty and sexual appeal, you are a Lover brand. However, food categories that offer unusual indulgences are also in this archetype.

In your marketing seek to develop deeper relationships with your customers. This is a much deeper and fuller connection than the connectivity wanted by the Regular Guy. You will need to express honesty, vulnerability, and passion.

It is also important to understand the relationship your customers have with your products, as this deeper connection will have unseen implications: your customers may associate your product with their personal relationships with family, friends, and lovers. If those relationships sour, so may the attraction to your product. Will you go back to your favorite restaurant after a break-up?

Lover brands

Fairmont Hotels, Hallmark Cards, eHarmony, Virginia (is for Lovers), Chanel, and Revlon.

Jester

The Marx Brothers, Will Rogers, Jay Leno, Dr. Seuss, and Jon Stewart are all Jester archetypes. Jesters are the clowns, the tricksters, and jokers we all know. They love to play jokes, have fun, and most of all, they love breaking the rules and poking fun at life's absurdities.

The Jester's goal is to live in the moment and make the most of it. They want people to lighten up and have a great time. Boredom frightens them.

People attracted to Jester archetypes are drawn to humor, bright colors, and lots of action. Clever ads are the hallmark of a Jester brand, such as those from Geico or Richard Branson's Virgin.

The original court jester or fool was the only one who was allowed to contradict the king. Thus he spoke the truth. Jester brands have this same opportunity: to speak the truth but in a fun or clever way. They can speak out when other brands feel compelled to remain silent. Thus a Jester brand can be a good way to deal with unhealthy products.

In marketing as a Jester, bring out the kid in your customers. It isn't only about the jokes, but in getting everyone involved in the fun.

It is also a solution for products that have no obvious differentiation from their competition. The personality of the Jester becomes more important than features, especially with a product that is a commodity. This opens the opportunity for the Jester brand Virgin to poke fun at its more staid rival, British Airways.

Beware of the joke turning cruel and hurtful. This may work for some comedians, but isn't a healthy approach for a company brand.

Jester brands
Geico, Pepsi, IKEA, M&M's, 7-UP, Jack in the Box, Ben & Jerry's, and Cadbury Creme Egg.

Change Agents

Hero

John Wayne, Superman, Nelson Mandela, Martin Luther King, Jr., Aung San Suu Kyi, Luke Skywalker, and Harry Potter are all heroes. Heroes fill our books and movies. They are the high energy people who act to change the world. They are willing to suffer defeat and risk death in order to take a stand and overcome obstacles, villains, and injustice.

Heroes are the champions of the underdog, and their goal is to protect others from harm or release them from injustice.

In marketing as a Hero archetype, consider using imagery where things are getting done, moving fast, or appearing powerful. Look for ways to demonstrate overcoming obstacles. Strong colors, lines, and shapes are appropriate. The hero gravitates to hard work and often austerity; he avoids comfort.

The Hero archetype is a natural for stories. Stories about passion, convictions, and overcoming obstacles are effective ways to communicate to those drawn to the Hero. People attracted to Heroes are looking for convictions and values that often seem missing in today's society. Cause-related marketing and social responsibility are part of the Hero archetype.

The Hero brand may be a company that has an innovation with major impact on the world, especially one that addresses environmental or social problems. Can your product do a tough job well? Are you the underdog who is challenging the status quo or a rival? Do your customers view themselves as people with good moral values? Then the Hero archetype might be a good fit.

If your brand, like Nike or the Marines, helps people be all they can be, you are a natural Hero brand.

Heros must be able to fulfill their archetype and never falter. Lance Armstrong was a Hero for overcoming cancer, winning the Tour de France seven times, and founding a foundation for cancer support. Overcoming all these physical and mental challenges set him up as a true Hero. However, the news that he used banned performance-enhancing drugs was a serious blow. He might have been able to maintain his Hero status, but the fact he lied about the drug use, coupled with his aggressive tactics in maintaining the cover-up, have seriously damaged his Hero archetype.

Hero brands
Apple's 1984 ad, U.S. Army, Nike, Federal Express, the Red Cross, and the U.S. Marines.

Rebel

Robin Hood, Zorro, Jack Nicholson, Che Guevara, Muhammad Ali, James Dean in *Rebel Without a Cause*, and Norma Rae are all Rebels.

The Rebel (or Outlaw) archetype desires revenge or revolution. The goal is to destroy what is not working. Destruction, disruption, or shock is usually the strategy.

Steve Jobs is considered a Creative archetype, but you can also consider him a Rebel for his individualistic style and often disruptive technologies.

Rebels can have a romantic and positive side, like Robin Hood, as they attempt to disrupt a society they see as corrupt. Butch Cassidy and the Sundance Kid also fit into this more romantic side of the Rebel.

The darker side of the Rebel can be seen in Internet hackers who create denial-of-service attacks on web sites or networks they want to disrupt to bring attention to a cause. These attacks may have a good cause at the core, but will have seriously negative repercussions for many innocent web site owners and users. The dark side of the Rebel is usually not a useful brand archetype, except in very specific situations and with careful management.

The Rebel may not be as universally admired as the Caregiver, but it definitely has its appeal for people looking to challenge the establishment. Harley Davidson is a great example of this.

In marketing, dark, shadowy qualities, and intense colors are used. You need to demonstrate a bit of contempt for the rules and cultural norms. You go for shock value with racy or edgy qualities in your marketing and customer interaction. A good way to reach people who appreciate the Rebel is through special interest publications. Rebels do not often read mainstream magazines.

Brands may use the Rebel as a way to add spice to their marketing.

Outlaw brands
Harley Davidson, MTV, Captain Morgan rum, Capital One (What's in Your Wallet?).

Magician

Merlin, Dolly Levi (*Hello, Dolly!*), Yoda, Mary Poppins, Willy Wonka, and Tony Robbins are Magicians.

Magicians heal the heart, mind, and body. They promise to help us find the fountain of youth or a magic wand. They make our dreams come true.

Magicians have great powers of perception and make things happen beyond what we thought was possible.

As a Magician brand you should look for ways to promise to transform your customer, either physically or emotionally (or both). This archetype appeals to New Age consumers and also cultural creatives. You always need to be selling yourself and your values when marketing yourself as a Magician.

Be sure that you have total alignment of your company, your employees, your products, and your marketing, or customers will see through the charade and you are doomed.

The Magician archetype fits companies with transformative products or services (weight loss, cosmetic procedures, personal growth, business success), those with a spiritual component, or a new and very contemporary product. This archetype allows you to price your services at the upper range due to its special appeal and promise.

Magician brands
Mr. Clean, Disneyland, Weight Watchers, genetic engineering firms, MasterCard and its Priceless campaign, Xbox, and Oil of Olay.

Archetypes and Ideal Customers

After reviewing the 12 archetypes discussed here, you may have yours identified. If not, then you may need to do some research on archetypes. Use the resources listed in Chapter 10 to dig deeper into these archetypes, as well as others that are related to these 12.

In addition, there are two websites that offer free online services to identify your archetype based on a short survey you complete. See Chapter 10 for their URLs. Even if you are confident of your selection, using the online tools is a good confirmation step and may open your eyes to other possibilities.

Once your archetype is defined, you need to identify what about this archetype will be most attractive to your ideal customers. In some cases, the answers are obvious, and steps to tightly align your brand with your archetype are straightforward. In other cases, you may need to rethink your brand strategy in order to fully leverage the power of your archetype.

Aligning to an archetype is a very powerful marketing tool, but you need to be sure you define the correct one for your ideal customers and implement it fully. You may need to interview customers, discuss your ideas with graphic artists, talk to packaging experts, and then test your ideas on customers before you leap into action. This is time well spent as you cannot easily change your archetype. If you try to change archetypes, you will look like a split personality and send the wrong message to all your current and desired customers.

Your goal is to build your archetype into the DNA of your company. It is not a suit of clothes that you put on. It is who you are, not a mask you wear.

Your Archetype

What is your brand archetype?

Review your signature story in terms of your archetype.

Does your archetype shine through?

What can you do to strengthen the archetype?

Do you need to change any elements of your existing marketing materials?

Do you need a new story to fit your archetype?

Document all the attributes of your archetype that you can use in stories and related marketing:

- Logo
- Tag line
- Words
- Colors
- Layout
- Writing tone of voice
- Examples
- Imagery
- Metaphors
- Product/Service descriptions
- Terms of Service, Legal, Policy pages
- Forms
- Email messages, autoresponders, and confirmation messages

REFINING YOUR STORIES

By now you should have a few stories written or at least in draft mode. Perhaps you also have some ideas for future stories. Now it is time to take your skills up a notch. In this chapter we will add other elements to make your stories more exciting.

In Chapter 3 we saw the story of my knee pain. The version in that chapter was a chronology of all the related events (doctor visits, therapy sessions, tests, etc.), and we discussed how we could use different elements of that narrative to support different messages. Different messages would require us to delete certain events, as they are not relevant to every message and would just be a distraction.

However, the final story was rather flat. Very little drama and, although it did support the message, it didn't create the emotional impact it could have.

The slavish following of the story arc alone obviously does not guarantee drama or even an enjoyable story. Writing is an art form. It is now time to look at other aspects of story writing in order to create stories people enjoy hearing.

Choices

Always remember this is your story, and its success depends on the choices you make.

Stories are not just a recitation of the events in a chronological sequence. When you write a story, you will select those events that are meaningful to your audience, work with the situation at hand, and support your message.

The choices you make in crafting your story work together to determine its impact.

When you make your choices, remember that stories are ways to share wisdom and not a recitation of facts.

Facts are what happened; truth is the meaning behind the facts. Facts tend to be permanent and verifiable. Truth in storytelling is more about values and may be dependant on the situation. Your stories are about truth, not facts. In my story, does it make any difference which medical professionals I went to? Or if I visited two doctors or three? Or which knee hurt? No. The truth of the story, that going with the least invasive remedy was the best approach, is still true. Be sure you select those elements that support the truth of your story.

Medium

We have been discussing written stories, but you may also be creating stories that will be spoken, perhaps stories to use at networking events. Before you start to craft your story, know which medium you plan to use. You may need both: a written version for the company newsletter and an oral version for your new hire orientation. The process will be different for written stories than oral ones.

Your oral story will allow you to use intonation, body language, props, sound effects, and other features that will create a very difference experience for your listeners than your readers. Take advantage of all the options an oral story situation provides.

Narrator and perspective

There is no such thing as an objectively told story. Your narrator and point of view are choices you will make, and they can significantly impact your story.

Who is telling the story? Often it will be you, but you may speak from the perspective of another person. This perspective could be yours (as the owner), or a customer's, an employee's,

NOTES

NOTES

_____
_____
_____
_____
_____
_____
_____
_____
_____
_____
_____
_____
_____
_____
_____
_____
_____
_____
_____
_____
_____
_____
_____
_____
_____
_____

or even a competitor's. Your point of view will reflect your age, gender, experience, culture, worldview, and the archetype of the business.

Notice how the story of Uncle Hiromichi in Chapter 9 is a conversation. Eavesdropping on another conversation is much more intriguing than just hearing a third party retell that same conversation. Look for opportunities to include conversations.

Characters

In most stories, you will have one or at most two characters. Most stories are too short to have any more without confusing the reader. Is each of these characters necessary to the story? Is she a real person or a composite?

Describing a specific person may be too limiting, but a composite built of several people may give the story broader relevancy and fills in voids that would be present if you only included one specific factual character.

For example, my story of Jennifer in the Preface is really a composite. One client was the inspiration for this story, and I changed her name for privacy reasons. Then I added details from other clients who experienced the same situations "Jennifer" did. We are back to the fact vs. truth decision. For my message "truth" conveyed through a composite character was the correct choice.

Chronology

When writing a story we can often get in a rut by repeating the events in their chronological order. My knee pain story is just a recitation of I did this, then he did that, etc. This can make for a boring story as each event has the same prominence. It is like speaking in a monotone.

Starting in the middle, using flashbacks or flashforwards are chronology techniques you should consider.

See "About the Power of Psychotactics" in Chapter 9. The author opens with his first job, then flashes back to his parents and growing up, and then moves forward to today.

In addition, not every event needs the same weight in the story. You can pace your stories by having some events get more attention, while others get only a brief mention.

Emotional arc

We talked about the story arc in Chapter 3, but there is also an emotional arc in play that might be more useful for your story. The emotional arc is concerned with how you as the narrator (or your readers) feel about the events in your story.

Going back to the knee pain story, perhaps I want to play up the uncertainty I had about having an MRI and my claustrophobia. What if I didn't really want this test done and was fighting the urge to ignore the doctor's request for the test because I feared the results and felt that what I didn't know wouldn't hurt me?

If this inner struggle was important to this version of the story, I would downplay the details of the doctor visits and therapy sessions, and spend more time drawing out this inner conflict. I could describe my fears in getting ready to go to the hospital, my inattentive driving due to my distraction of the upcoming test, my shaking as the MRI machine made horrifying banging noises, and finally the anxiety as I waited for the test results.

None of this was in the original version of the story. Chronologically, this episode was before the climax of the original story. Using the emotional arc approach, the events following the MRI, (including the story's plot climax) would be minimized.

As the writer you have complete control over which elements get the dramatic treatment. Spend time playing around with the emotional arc to see if your story improves.

Build a Story

A creative way to play with your plot sequences, story arcs, and emotional arcs is with sticky notes.

Get a pad of those little yellow notes and write each of the events on a separate note. Have a note for each trigger or change of direction in the action.

If you have an artistic bent, you may want to draw the events rather than just writing the words.

Place all the notes on a piece of paper or wall or any surface you have. You are building a storyboard for your story. Now start rearranging your story sequence. Put the beginning first, try flashbacks and flash forwards, remove some parts of the action, and perhaps add other details to shift the emotional arc.

Take all the notes and turn them blank side up. Rearrange them randomly and then turn them over. Can you construct a convincing story out of this random sequence?

The goal of this exercise is to see how many ways you can rearrange the story, and to uncover interesting perspectives, messages, and drama that are hidden in your basic story.

NOTES

_____

_____

_____

_____

_____

_____

_____

_____

_____

_____

_____

_____

_____

_____

_____

_____

_____

_____

_____

_____

_____

_____

Tension

In addition to the main conflict situations in a story, there may be underlying tension, or a pull, between characters or opposing forces. This is not necessarily negative, and it does not have physical action. For example, it might be a customer who is in fear of losing important company data, or a customer service employee who doesn't know how to respond to an angry customer.

If this tension is important to the story, be sure to give it the prominence it needs.

The Story Audit

The whole story

Review the following facets of your story as a whole before you start looking at individual elements.

Message is clear
Know exactly what message you want to communicate. Is it obvious? Is there only one message, or are you trying to do too much with one story?

Conflict is believable
Are the conflict situations appropriate? If your story is too dramatic people may not be able to connect with it.

Characters resonate
Are the villain (if present) and hero easy to identify with? Is the struggle to reach the goal believable? Is it a struggle the ideal customer will appreciate?

Plot holds interest
The flow of events are vital to your ideal customer's interests. Is there a clear trigger for the change in action? Are there enough events to be interesting? Events should be paced from

introduction through a variety of conflict scenes to climax and resolution. Of course, in a shorter story there will not be enough time for too many conflict points.

Story builds on what they already know

Stories work best when the reader already is aware of many of the details, and only a portion (usually your solution) is new. Review your story to make sure that you are not introducing too many obscure words or concepts. Do you connect with the reader's problem or situation before you start talking about your solution?

Individual story elements

Next review the individual aspects of your story for places to improve it.

Hooks the reader through the title

Not all stories have titles or headlines, but if yours does, spend significant time developing it. A boring title promises a boring story.

Builds on the reader's attention with the opening

The title got her interest, now the opening must keep it. It must compel her to keep reading to find out how the story ends. Does it?

Moves the story quickly into the conflict

Don't drag out the introduction with too many extraneous details. The reader is only interested if the story applies to her. So don't bog things down with information that is not pertinent to your reader. This is a common problem, but it can easily be overcome if you are always thinking about your message and your reader.

Builds momentum and tension with just enough conflict

In a novel or a movie script there are many subplots, plot twists, and conflict situations. You are not writing a novel. You are communicating a business message to a reader who is challenged for time and needs to solve a problem.

Revisit A Story

Now would be a good time to take one of the stories you have written and apply the audit to it.

Can you find places where you can make it better?

Do this exercise every day or at least 3 times a week until you have reviewed all your stories.

The goal is to get in the practice of auditing a story so that it becomes second nature.

NOTES

_____
_____
_____
_____
_____
_____
_____
_____
_____
_____
_____
_____
_____
_____
_____
_____
_____
_____
_____
_____
_____
_____
_____
_____
_____
_____
_____

The amount of conflict must be appropriate to the story. On your *About Us* page you can spend as much time as you like. Be sure to liberally use subheads, bullets, and boldface text so the reader can easily move through the story. Some testimonials may be quite long and still be effective. Yes, you are telling a story. But remember that you are not an entertainer (well, unless that is your archetype and that style fits with what you are selling), so staying on point is important.

Has good transitions between paragraphs

One paragraph should clearly flow to the next one. Connect the paragraphs with repeated words or concepts.

Liberal use of subheads is desirable as they help pull the reader along through the story.

See *About the Power of Psychotactics* in Chapter 9 for the use of subheads and good transitions between paragraphs.

Applies the disconnect principle sparingly

Sometimes you don't want each paragraph to flow neatly from one to the other. Especially in a longer story, it is good to have a quick break, an unexpected thought, or new development. If done intentionally and well, this can add a dramatic element to the story and be very effective.

Uses lively words

Review all the sentences for passive words, such as is, be, was, etc. Can you find more active words? What about empty words like "interesting"? This lazy word doesn't really provide any information to the reader. Replace it with a more descriptive word.

Avoid hollow words. Quality service, world class, awesome, professional, ground breaking, dynamic, paradigm, and innovative are all over-used and have lost their meaning and their punch. **Don't tell me** you have great service; **show me** through your stories.

Rewrite to avoid limp sentences and passive voice. Use more active, descriptive, and unusual words. Be mindful of your archetype. If you are a Caregiver, you will be using softer words than ones appropriate for a Rebel. But there are still energetic words that can make your writing emotional and memorable.

Varies sentence length and structure.
Are all your sentences the same length? Are they all subject-verb-object? This can bring a very dull tempo to your writing. Look for ways to break it up. Sprinkle in some short, punchy sentences. Break longer sentences into two for impact. Add subheads.

See Chapter 9 for the "The Great Chef and the Failing Restaurant" story which is a good example of using short sentences and short paragraphs (perhaps only one sentence long) for dramatic effect. When you are telling a story, you can pause for dramatic effect. When you are writing, you need to employ the visual cues of the text layout to provide this dramatic intention. As the writer, you are free to be as creative as you like with the visual layout of your story.

Aligns with your archetype
Review your archetype guidelines. Are you using appropriate words, phrases, and imagery to solidify your archetype?

Reflects back to the opening
A very useful technique is to open with an anecdote or interesting comment and then bring the story back to it at the end.

See "Why Black Tea Needs to Be Steeped in Boiling Water" in Chapter 9 for how the author circles back to the Ramen noodles at the end.

This technique isn't mandatory, but it is a device you should have in your story writing toolkit.

Is clear
Nothing beats clarity. You can have sparkling language, dramatic sentences, powerful characters, and compelling plot. But if your story isn't clear, you are sunk.

NOTES

NOTES

_____
_____
_____
_____
_____
_____
_____
_____
_____
_____
_____
_____
_____
_____
_____
_____
_____
_____
_____
_____
_____
_____
_____
_____
_____
_____
_____
_____
_____

Passes the read-aloud test

Reading aloud brings a new dimension to your story. You will notice the tempo and alliteration, and how well the words fit together. Adjust the wording of the story and sentence structure so it reads well aloud.

Passes the test of time

As you work on a story, it is too easy to get attached to specific words or sentences. You fall in love with your prose. Let it sit a bit and re-read it to put some distance between you-the-creator and you-the-reader. It is surprising how different the story will sound.

On the flip side, you may have thought that the story was dismal and were ready to trash it. Don't. Wait a few days an re-read it. You may be surprised at how good it really is. Or, after letting the story marinate for a bit, you will be able to quickly spot a problem that can be easily fixed and will transform the story.

Survives a second opinion

Having someone else give you feedback is a great idea. This works best when it is someone you trust, and who is really giving honest feedback, not just telling you it is great because they think that is what you want to hear. Another approach is to seek someone who is not familiar with the story. Fresh ears are a good test of your story.

The best way to get useful feedback is to ask specific questions. Don't just ask, "Did you like it?" Instead, think about the message you are trying to convey and the action you want the reader to take. Does your test reader feel the story would compel her to take that action? Is there something missing? Something confusing?

You Are Done!

Put your finished masterpiece away where you can use it as needed. But remember that stories are living creatures and they will evolve over time.

NOTES

7 BUILDING YOUR BRAND THROUGH STORIES

purpose story

passion story

product names

social media

staff bios

culture story

blog posts

hang tags

testimonials

package inserts

new hire kit

customer success stories

elevator pitch

networking events

What is a Story-Based Brand?

A quick Google search will bring up thousands of articles touting "build your brand story." To be precise, the search I just did for that phrase brought up 171,000 results. Without the quotes, I now have 46,800,000 pages to wade through. Clearly, story-based branding is a hot marketing topic.

Start reviewing the individual listings, and you quickly realize that, rather than finding articles with advice you can use to create a story-based brand, you have link after link to pages that fall into two camps:

♦ Articles that serve as inspiration for a CEO or marketing executive with a team of in-house staff or hired consultants to do the heavy lifting.
♦ Articles promoting a single idea: all you need is one great brand story. Get that one story out there and you are set.

The first problem is that you may be the entire team. Without a road map on how you can create and use these stories, you have a great idea but no way to implement it. You need practical steps you can take, as there are no ad agency or marketing department resources you can call on.

Secondly, one great brand story is not enough. In this book we are not talking about a single big brand story that you can drag out for your *About Us* page, your trade show booth, or your new employee orientation, but otherwise never makes an appearance in the rest of your marketing and company operations.

To truly benefit from stories and build a story-based brand, you need to weave stories throughout your

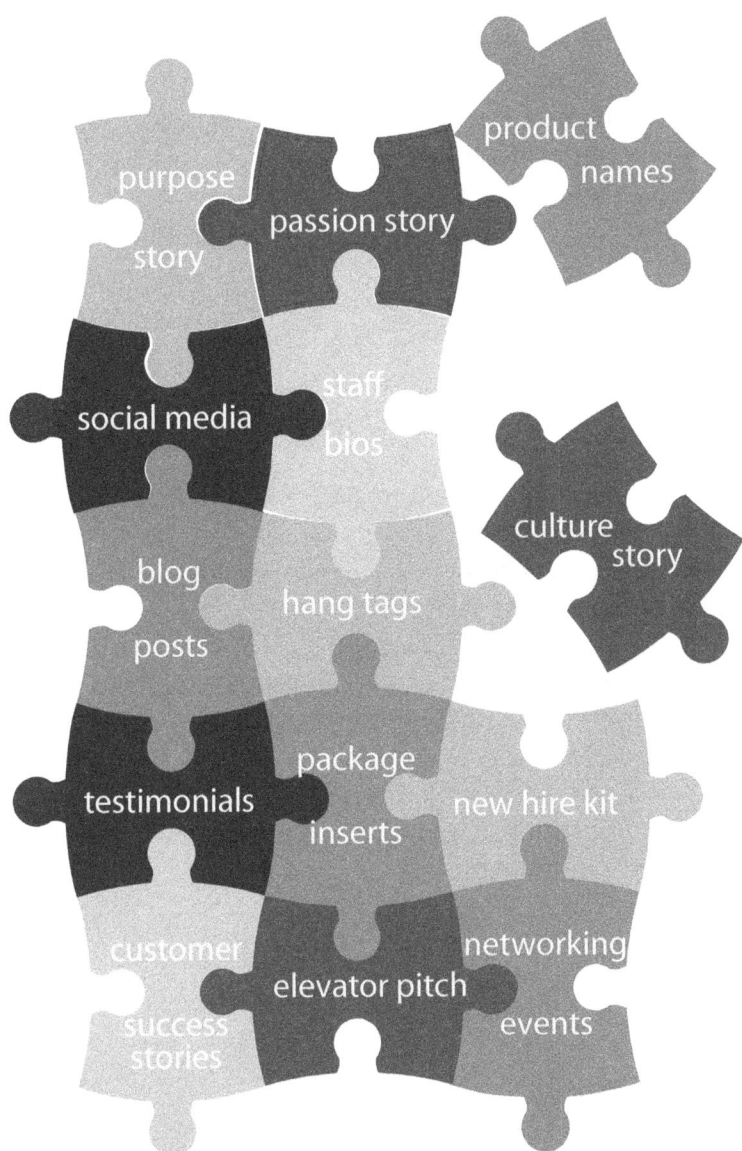

company culture (internal stories) and your marketing (external stories).

The one big brand story is not only ineffective, it can give the world the impression you are doing little more than window dressing.

Guidelines for Using Stories

Before we get into where to use stories, it would be good to review some basic guidelines:

- Use stories appropriately. Not everything you want to communicate should be—or can be—in story form.
- Always start crafting your story with the message you want to convey. Stories are not fluff. They are always designed to intentionally impart specific messages about your business.
- Eliminate all extraneous parts of the story that are not focused on driving the message.
- Stories are not a chronology. You do not need every step in the process (I did this and then I did that, ad nauseam). Keep the story crisp and focused on the message. You may even rearrange the sequence to add drama to the story.
- Your core story sets the stage for your brand. All other stories—and non-story marketing—flow from this foundation. The core story sets your archetype, your values, your tone of voice, your imagery. Stay true to this with all your marketing.
- For greatest impact, your story must have the four core story elements.
- Anecdotes are not necessarily stories, but they are useful parts of your marketing. They may not fit the true definition—and thus not have the full power—of a story, but will still have great emotional impact on the reader. They will also be aligned with, and support, your other stories.

Where Are You Now?

The first step in moving to a story-based brand is to know your starting point. Print web pages, plus other online marketing samples, and gather all the print materials you have so you can review as a whole. Keep notes on multimedia efforts, such as videos, to complete the picture.

Get started with:

- Web site: Home, About Us, Testimonials, Product and Services pages.
- Blog
- Videos, both on web site and YouTube or other video outlets
- Facebook posts
- Podcasts
- Newsletter samples
- Print brochures
- Flyers
- Email signatures and answering machine messages.
- Internal documents, such as training documents and safety manuals.

This list is just to get you started. You may have many other marketing elements you need to collect. The goal is to have them in one place, so you can review for story opportunities, as well as spotting breaks in your brand consistency.

Your Bedrock Stories

Right now jot down some ideas for the following stories:

Business Founding Story

Your Passion Story Why do you care so much about this business?

Your Purpose Story Why do you do what you do? What is your mission?

Your Positioning Story How do you want your customers to perceive your business relative to the competition?

Your Personality How will people experience your brand? Serious and stable? Fun? Quirky? Irreverent? Inspiring?

Four Types of Stories

Stories, written or spoken, can be grouped into four categories: Bedrock, Opportunity Knocks, Hip-Pocket, and Inside Stories. The first three are considered external facing. You tell these to customers, prospects, investors, partners, etc. Inside Stories are used with your employees: for motivation, training, and culture-building.

But there is much cross over; don't get too focused on categorizing stories. The categories are used to help us discuss types of stories in an organized way and are not meant as a road block to creative uses of your stories. As long as the message of the story is right for the audience and the situation, you should use it.

Bedrock stories

These are the foundational stories—usually formal, written stories—of your business. These stories appear on your web site and in brochures, and are used to explain your company and your brand.

John Jantsch of Duct Tape Marketing refers to these as the "Four Stories Every Business Must Build":

- Your Passion Story
- Your Purpose Story
- Your Positioning Story
- Your Personality Story

Bedrock stories may be built around your company founding or its mission. They might be company legends: Harland David Sanders (Colonel Sanders of KFC) and his many failures before finding the right recipe for his chicken, or Steve Jobs and Steve Wozniak building computers in the garage, or internal stories told for employee motivation and culture-building.

Bedrock stories are ones you should start writing now. Start compiling a list of these required stories, so you can develop them later, as needed.

Opportunity knocks stories

These are stories that arise in the course of doing business with customers and partners. Always be on the alert for these stories. Many great stories are lost because the listener had not developed the story muscles to recognize a good story and its value.

As you develop a heightened awareness for stories you will automatically recognize:
- A great story when you hear it (and will write it down)
- A missed opportunity because you had no story with the needed message (and will start to search for a story to fill this need)

Stories that overcome objections or prove the value of your service fall in this category. Keeping a notebook handy (or a cell phone with dictation ability) will allow you to note these opportunities as they happen. You cannot rely on your memory!

Hip pocket stories

These are oral stories you can whip out on demand to fill many needs. They can save situations where you might otherwise be at a loss for words. Frequent telling of these stories means they can be used with ease so you appear full of confidence. If needed, they can take the spotlight off you and put it on a customer's success.

Hip-Pocket stories are often overlooked in favor of the more polished Bedrock stories. But they are vital to a fully story-based brand. These Hip-Pocket stories act as credibility factors. They are the supporting players for your marketing. With such a robust cache of stories, you build confidence that all your stories are authentic.

We have all encountered a business that has a great story about its founding or its mission, but our personal experiences may not align with that story. This happens when stories are built as

Opportunity Habits

Opportunity stories are everywhere, but without a habit of collecting them, memory of them will vanish.

What can you do to make sure everyone in your organization is on the lookout for story opportunities? How are you saving these stories for easy retrieval?

1.

2.

3.

4.

5.

6.

Inside Stories

If you have employees, think how you can use stories to motivate, train, and enlighten your staff. Review these ideas to start planning where you need to develop stories.

Hiring process
Are there stories to tell during the interview process that will help an applicant know if you are a good match for her?

New hire training
What stories can you tell to educate a new hire on how you work? Communicate safety procedures? Introduce the latitude an employee may have with customers?

Team building
Are employees encouraged to share their stories, such as how they made a difficult sale?

Do you create stories from your company events?

Sharing of company culture
How can you share your company culture? Do you put stories in the employee newsletter or internal blog? Do you post stories on the bulletin board?

Are employees encouraged to share their stories of their values and goals?

Are you reinforcing your stories at company meetings on a regular basis? Are you frequently adding to your library of company stories?

a marketing effort and not integrated into the fabric of the business. They are just a facade.

Don't let this happen to your business. If all your employees know your Bedrock stories and also have a handy supply of Hip-Pocket stories, they will be authentically representing your brand.

One bonus of Hip-Pocket stories? The power of story to improve memory can work for the storyteller as well as the listener! Never be at a loss for words when dealing with a customer, a vendor, or a journalist. You know your stories. Just tell them.

Inside stories

Inside Stories are for you and your staff. Many will be used only within the organization, but some may have external uses as well. Just be clear which is which!

By having "internal only" stories, you not only strengthen the idea that these are bonding stories, you also welcome stories of failure, turnaround, challenges, and even competition.

Internal stories can be used during the hiring process to help people feel comfortable or to help them judge if your business is right for them. You will be able to evaluate the applicant's reaction to your stories.

When I was a new college graduate on the job hunt, I was invited back East for an interview with a national consumer foods brand. I was thrilled by this opportunity and, of course, doing my best to impress the interviewer. However, during the course of the day-long ordeal, the interviewer starting talking about the yearly sensitivity retreats for all employees. These were probably valuable off-site team building events, but the way he described them made me (a total introvert) feel extremely uncomfortable. I began to seriously doubt if I could thrive in such an environment. They were not the company for me.

New employees will benefit from stories told by managers and colleagues as they get settled in. Stories can be effective training and bonding tools. No new employee should be given a written employee manual and left to her own devices. These culture-building stories will create immediate and long-lasting bonds.

Internal storytelling does not end after the new hire orientation. Use stories for motivation, ongoing training, new product introductions, and overall company cultural reinforcement.

Stories are very effective in demonstrating how much latitude employees have in making decisions. You could develop a list of rules for dealing with unsatisfied customers, but how much more effective would it be to just tell a story?

Zappos, the online shoe store, has a core value of "Deliver WOW through Service." What does WOW service look like? Where would you even begin to define all the attributes of WOW service? Zappos uses actual employee stories to share their WOW moments to illustrate what this means in a way that no documentation could ever accomplish. You can order a free copy of their annual *Zappos Culture Book* to see this for yourself. See Chapter 10 for details on how to obtain your own copy.

Moving to a Story-Based Brand

As you start writing your stories, you will end up with a collection of stories, but wonder how they can work together to create a story-based brand.

You may notice that some of your stories are big and bold (perhaps your passion story), and others may be smaller in scope. Some get used all the time, while others only make an appearance in select settings. Then we have supporting elements to the stories that show up as needed. These other elements, such as logos, colors,

Objections and Stories

Using your testimonials to overcome objections is such a valuable way to use stories. List your common objections and then identify a customer who had that objection, still bought, and was happy. Then write her story.

Objection #1

Customer

Objection #2

Customer

Objection #3

Customer

Objection #4

Customer

Objection #5

Customer

Your Stage Hands

How are you using stage hands? Try to use as many senses as possible. What will appeal to your ideal customers. Spa patrons may expect and appreciate the aroma of lavender. If you are selling truck tires, fragrance might not work.

Images and colors

Textures

Fragrances

Sounds

Flavors

design elements, jingles, etc., express your archetype, personality, and brand promise while they continue the story line. When you are working on all of these pieces, and especially if you are working without an experienced brand designer, it may seem overwhelming and your efforts unorganized.

You may feel you have a lot of pieces, but they are not working together. Those pieces do not seem to add up to a well-executed brand.

An easy way to clear this confusion is to think about a live theater production. There will be a writer, a producer, financial backer, starring cast, supporting players, sets, costumes, props, music, and more. Looked at individually, this is a complex and disparate group of contributors (just like your marketing stories and graphic elements). But combined appropriately, and with a single goal, they become a great theater experience.

We can group these various contributors to a theater production into three categories that also apply to a great story-based brand:
- stars
- supporting players
- stage hands

Stars

Stars are your core brand stories that have the required story elements. Your creation and passion stories are here. These are the foundational stories that the other, smaller ones, support. If you are an organic bakery, then you have a foundation story of how you came to organic foods (perhaps including overcoming an illness) and your passion for organic baked goods. The stories of your individual products and how they came to be will all be supporting this central theme.

Supporting players

Most of your stories will be supporting players. These will be product stories, customer testimonials, training stories, and the like that build on and reinforce your core star stories. Supporting players may be true stories or anecdotes, narratives, or other communication.

Narratives and anecdotes are missing one or more of the story elements. However, they contain enough emotional detail to enable the listener to create her own mental picture. They are not necessarily as powerful (from a brain perspective) as a story, but they are very useful in building your brand engagement with your ideal customer.

Take a look at the J. Peterman (www.jpeterman. com/) product descriptions. Not all elements of the story form are present so these qualify as anecdotes. However, enough emotional detail is present that they engage the reader, and they continue the brand personality established through the core stories and the brand archetype.

Also look at Trader Joe's Fearless Flyer. (www. traderjoes.com/fearless-flyer/). These are mostly entertaining anecdotes, but they are very effective in getting the reader interested in buying the product. As with J. Peterman, they reinforce the brand personality.

Stage hands

Stage hands are non-story elements that continue the story line. Think of these like props, music sets, and costumes in a play. They are important to support the story, but they are not the story.

These stage hands are sensory elements to reinforce your brand. They could be images, sounds, flavors, colors, textures, or fragrances. They reference the same characters, situations, or struggles

NOTES

NOTES

contained in your stories. They are your brand colors and tone of voice.

Some stage hands can become icons that seem to have a life of their own. Think of Dorothy's ruby slippers, Harry Potter's invisibility cloak, the smell of fresh-baked Cinnabon rolls piped through the mall HVAC ducts, or the opening notes in the theme from *Jaws*.

Stage hands are ways to keep the story weaving through all of your marketing. Stage hands support your customer experience and express your archetype, and therefore help fulfill your brand promise.

As stage hands complete the user experience, they should be used wherever possible. Examples of places to use stage hands are:

+ hang tags
+ business cards
+ package inserts
+ product names
+ instruction labels
+ store signage
+ newspaper ads

Every place you touch a customer is an opportunity to include a stage hand.

Stage hands may sound like incidental elements in your marketing, but that would seriously underestimate their power. These sensory elements are as critical to your brand as songs are to a musical.

You may need to work with your graphic designer, web developer, copywriter, or other specialists to help you incorporate these stage hand elements. But don't let the need for this effort derail your story writing. The stories come first—the non-story elements support the stories.

Using Your Stories

It is time to take your collection of stories and ideas, and start assigning them to all your marketing materials.

The easiest way to get started is to cherry-pick those places that are ready-made for story in your existing marketing, rather than trying to do an entire overhaul. As you go through this exercise, you will begin to get additional story ideas. Listen to these thoughts—they are your emerging story muscles starting to work.

Web Site *About Us* Page

This is an obvious story opportunity. On your *About Us* page you are free to be as creative as possible. Avoid the stodgy, safe route of a timeline. Don't work at being impressive. The goal is to be real, to be human. People will expect to see your personality emerge here. Give it to them.

Staff biographies

Depending on your brand personality, you have full creative license here. Avoid the stale resume style biography. Yes, you will want to include educational background, awards, and certifications, but these can be listed at the end. First, get the reader's attention with a great story.

Ask staff members to identify stories that encapsulate who they are. Thinking back over their lives, were there any epiphanies? Failures that gave them insight? Challenges that set them on a new—and better—course? A tough decision they made, but made for the right reason? An insight to their core values?

Overcoming objections

This is the mother lode of opportunity. Every time you hear an objection, you should immediately get into story mode. Unless you just

NOTES

NOTES

opened your doors yesterday, you will have a stockpile of objections. Every objection should have a story that shows how a customer overcame it or could overcome it.

Push-back on price? Tell the story of a customer who hesitated because of price but bought anyway and benefited. The best stories of overcoming price objections will have specific benefits the customer obtained (dollars saved through eliminating maintenance costs, dollars gained with increased revenues), not just generic "They loved it."

Do this with every objection you have heard, as well as those you know they are thinking but haven't yet voiced. Stories to overcome objections may be one of the most potent ways to use stories.

Testimonial Strategy

This is a good time to rethink your testimonial strategy. Do you have a wait-and-hope approach to testimonials? You just wait and hope that someone will say something nice in an email or on Yelp?

If that is your strategy, you are losing on two fronts: the number of testimonials and the quality of the ones you do get. A better strategy is to interview your customers, find out if they had any initial objections, and then turn those into testimonial stories.

Customer case studies

Customer success stories are quite persuasive. Not only are they a natural to put into story form, but the idea of a real customer sharing their experience adds credibility that is hard to get any other way.

Do not think that these need to be formal documents; customer case studies can be short and informal. They just need to be authentic, offer a message that is useful for the reader, and in keeping with your brand.

Newsletter articles

If you have a company newsletter, you know how difficult it can be to write something for each issue. Take a cue from newspaper journalists to make your life easier: start with a story.

When you are writing for your own newsletter, always think first in terms of message: what am I trying to communicate? Then see if there is a story that can become the starting point for the article.

Blog posts

Although blog posts can be considered shorter and more casual than full articles, the same principles apply. However, you don't need to have a story for every blog post. If a story will get your point across, use one. But don't force it or think that you must have a story every time you have something to say. But as you get stronger story-writing skills, you may find that stories just come naturally.

Social media

This is where you can really go crazy with stories. Whether you use YouTube, Facebook, Twitter, Pinterest, other social channels, or all of the above, stories can drive your content.

Yes, many Facebook posts will be product announcements or sales events or other straightforward communications. But, stories should be included in the mix. Stories on Facebook allow you to get feedback (comments and shares) that show your customers want to hear from you.

It isn't just about you talking to customers. Encourage people to share their stories on these channels. Once again, this is an ideal way to do some market research. And, it is a great customer service opportunity. Use it.

NOTES

NOTES

_____

_____

_____

_____

_____

_____

_____

_____

_____

_____

_____

_____

_____

_____

_____

_____

_____

_____

_____

_____

_____

_____

_____

_____

_____

If your customers are not using these social channels, you may not need to spend time there. But if they are, you should be there, telling stories to engage these customers and their network of friends.

The elevator pitch

Is there anyone who hasn't heard of the need for an elevator pitch? Probably not. But most guidelines for how to create one focus on getting in all the important details. Or they go the other extreme and advise that you create a "hook" that usually is disingenuous, but will get the listener to ask what you mean. Why not treat the listener with respect and give him a short story instead of a tease?

Networking events

Your elevator pitch is not enough; at a networking event you need to have those Hip-Pocket stories ready. You never know whom you will meet or what conversations you will be in. These are also wonderful places to get new story ideas.

Be on the alert for stories others are telling or for places where you didn't understand something (or didn't really care) and think if a story would have made a difference. A story might have explained the concept so you understood it, or it might have made you understand why you should be interested.

Use networking events as market (and story) research opportunities. Don't fear going because you hate small talk. Jump in and see what you can learn.

Welcome packets

Do you offer a package of materials to all new customers? These are often used to convey important information such as privacy policies, legal disclaimers, installation instructions, warranty information, and the like. This is the ideal place to add in some stories about using your products and engaging with your company.

Just after purchasing a product or service is a sensitive time for a buyer. She may be starting to reconsider her purchase. Do not let buyer's remorse enter into your customer's thoughts. Instead, you want her to feel confident she made the right choice. Providing stories of other happy customers will reinforce her buying decision. Include stories of the company, the person who shipped the product, and the customer service rep who can be called for help. Your stories can be the bridge from happy buyer to happy consumer of your products.

New product announcements

Explaining big or new concepts is a perfect place for a story. Use the story as a way to help people understand new technology or why the reader should care.

Whenever you are introducing a new idea, service, or product, look for a story that will get attention and set the context for your announcement. You may use a fictitious person with a problem and then demonstrate how your new product solves it. Your story will include enough details about this person to allow your reader to see herself in the story. The message will be obvious: she needs your product! Video stories can be especially convincing in these situations.

Product descriptions

Product descriptions are necessary, but often just the facts of size, weight, color, etc. If you are a reseller, you may routinely use the product descriptions provided by the manufacturer. This approach will not make your products memorable or enticing.

Online resellers may have an additional challenge because everyone else selling the same product now is using the same description. This doesn't help set your business apart in the eyes

NOTES

NOTES

of the buyer, and it is also a hurdle for good web search visibility for you.

The solution? You may not be able to tell a story for every product, but you can certainly include anecdotes and other story elements to make those product descriptions more interesting and memorable.

Take a look at the J. Peterman catalog. Those luscious descriptions have hooked many a browser into being a buyer. Trader Joe's markets and Duluth Trading also do a great job of using stories when discussing products. If you find a company that appeals to you, consider signing up for their newsletter or subscribing to their blog posts to see how they use stories. It doesn't have to be in a related industry; some of your best ideas will come from outside your industry.

Another example is as near as your local want ads: the pets for adoption section. Have you noticed how the ads have morphed from just the facts about the animal, to the facts plus a photo, and now to a photo and story? This is done for a reason: it works. So spend some time checking out the pets to adopt and get some story ideas for your products or services. Be careful you don't fall for one of these delightful stories and adopt a pet you don't need.

Packaging

Take a good look at your product packaging. Is it utilitarian and nothing more? Or does it continue to promote your brand promise?

Packaging can be a reinforcement to a buyer that she made the right choice. Look at the packaging used by Apple for its products. They are beautiful and elegant and a perfect fit for a design-focused company.

You can enhance your packaging by including written information (anecdotes and stories) with the product. Some consumer retailers include a handwritten note from the packer; others use pre-printed cards that thank you for buying. The package may include other elements, such as care instructions, other uses, or free samples of companion products.

It is easy to overlook the customer's relationship with your product when they have it at home and you are not there to observe. What happens when UPS delivers the box or the shopper arrives home with their purchases? Is your brand promise still in effect?

I used to subscribe to a book club service from a book seller in Ireland. It was a free-form sort of club where you identified subject areas and frequency, and magically a box would arrive on your doorstep with an assortment of books, selected just for you.

I loved this service. I would always leave the box unopened until I had quiet time to open the box and savor the experience.

I had a specific ritual for the box opening. The box came with Irish stamps so I would check those out first, then I would open the box and take out the newspaper pages that would be used as stuffing. It was always fun to read what was going on in the town, the hurling scores, and the local real estate listings. Each book was wrapped in paper—that paper that you can tell immediately is European, not American, and they were tied with string. Often there was a poem or art print as a bit of lagniappe. It was like Christmas.

One day a shipment arrived with no Irish stamps and a New Jersey postmark. Horrors! Cost cutting had come to my book club. I am sure this was a tactic to improve the thin margins in the book business, and in the face of the rising giant Amazon, it was no doubt necessary.

When I opened the box, it was clear my Irish book experience was over. The books were packed in plastic popcorn. No more Irish hurling scores for me! Ordinary paper covered the books. The whole experience was ruined. It wasn't long before I cancelled my subscription.

NOTES

NOTES

I am sure the bookseller had no idea what happened. They thought they were selling Irish books, but to me they were selling an Irish experience. They may have reduced costs, but they tossed out my experience with those costs. The had used stories effectively, including their family story, the founding of the bookstore, plus stories from others in the book club and how they valued the service. They just ignored that I had my own story about their service. When they eliminated that Irish experience and just focused on getting the books to me as cheaply as possible, they broke their brand promise to me and ended my story.

This story highlights two important points:
- Your customers may have rituals that are critical to their brand experience. It is equally critical for you to know what these are and honor them.
- If you are in the lifestyle products business or sell a discretionary product or service, people are often buying for the experience **and** the product. It is so easy for us to focus on the product or service, and not nurture the experience. Support your customers' need to extend your stories by adding their own.

Employee training

These are usually Inside Stories as we discussed earlier. Just don't leave them to chance.

Do you have a training manual? Or training seminars for new hires? Annual safety meetings for all staff? These are perfect places to insert stories. Look through your training materials for places you can use a story. Don't overlook including your current employees in tracking down these stories. Very often, there are stories that are already told on the factory floor or back room that you don't even know exist.

Product sales training

Product sales training can often be a total bore. Technical people are doing their best to explain the intricacies of a new device to an audience that just wants to get out and sell. Sales people are a notoriously difficult audience. They are used to controlling the situation, not being passive observers. Sitting in a meeting that someone else is running is unbearable to them.

But if you provide stories to your sales people, they will be interested and will see those stories as sales tools. It is a win-win. They will pay attention in the training, and they will have real tools they can use to exceed their sales quotas.

Often overlooked places

We are all good at identifying the obvious places for stories, like the *About Us* page and our networking meeting introduction. We are also good at making sure our logo, colors, brochures, etc. are aligned with our archetype. But as they say, the devil is in the details. Put your brand to the test by looking at all the little places that might be overlooked: for starters try these places:

- Listen to your recorded phone message
- Review your email signature
- Review your email out-of-the-office auto responder
- Sign up for your newsletter and review the confirmation page and the welcome email
- Unsubscribe from your newsletter and review the resulting "sorry to see you go" page
- Enter an invalid URL for a web page on your site and look at the resulting 404 error page
- If you use an automated customer service phone system, trying calling it with a fictitious problem
- Order one of your products, taking note of the entire order process and the resulting shipment

What were the results? Did they seamlessly express your archetype? Did they include any appropriate story elements? Or were you unaware, or had forgotten, that these customer

NOTES

touch points existed? These are just a few places that are easily forgotten that create cracks in your branding alignment and customer engagement.

Now is a good time to create a system to catch these little details and fix them. Also, educate your staff about the importance of consistent brand alignment when creating any new customer touch points.

Stories: A Warning

Once you have established your archetype and expressed your brand promise through your stories and story elements, it is critical that you never falter. Your business and stories must be authentic. You must never betray the trust of your customer.

One sad example of a brand failure is Kashi. Kashi built a brand around organic, whole grain foods and uses the tag line "7 whole grains on a mission."

Building on the "mission" theme, they produced ads of individual Kashi employees traveling the planet looking for little known grains that could be sustainably raised and create great whole grain products.

Their web site built on this theme with the line "Many of us at Kashi don't know where Kashi ends and we begin. To us, Kashi is more than products in packages—it's a way of life."

Unfortunately they used genetically modified (GMO) soybeans in some of their products, and this undisclosed fact was made public in a report from the Cornucopia Institute. Kashi was outed, and the backlash was severe.

Since then Kashi has tried to recover with videos explaining the situation; correcting widespread, incorrect information on the Internet; and promising to be GMO-free by 2015.

Charges and counter charges ensued. The company (now owned by Kellogg's) is engaged in full damage control. The story is still unfolding, so it is too soon to tell the long term implications for the brand.

To its credit, Kashi has developed a very robust anti-GMO campaign and is doing all it can to regain trust with its ideal customers.

Even if Kashi is successful, how much has it spent in money, time, and energy on this fire fighting? Could these resources have been better spent?

Kellogg's may have the money to do this; most small businesses do not. Even if you have the money for such a PR assault on behalf of your brand, do you really need the distraction?

The moral of this story: stay true to what your customers expect. Fulfill your brand promise. Anything else is brand suicide.

NOTES

GOING FORWARD

MOTIVATION + TRIGGER + ABILITY = HABIT

What Now?

You now know why stories can be magic for your marketing: **stories are the keys to Your Unstoppable Brand**.

You have written some stories, and they may be in various states from an idea, to an outline, to a draft, to a fully polished story.

You may have even put some of these stories on your web site or included them in a brochure. You might have tried out a few testimonial stories with a prospective customer.

It is probably too early to hope that your stories have radically improved your business, but it isn't too much to hope that you are seeing signs of change, just like new shoots coming up in the spring.

You have invested considerable time working through the book: reading, absorbing, brainstorming, and writing.

But now is the moment of truth: how are you going to keep this momentum going?

Yoda, the Sage archetype in *Star Wars*, was correct: "Try not. Do, or do not. There is no try."

The challenge for you is to define your next steps and to keep those story muscles that you have been developing on a continued path of growth.

Next Steps

Step #1 | Where are you going?

We started this journey with a review of your current marketing efforts and materials. Now is the time to update that analysis.

What has changed? What have you added? What new ideas do you have? Are any projects already underway?

Are you using a few stories in your marketing and think that is sufficient? Or are you committed to building a fully story-based brand?

If you have a larger organization, are you planning to use stories for training and culture building? Do you have team members who can start enhancing their story skills and who can spearhead this new movement within your organization?

Perhaps you have been thinking of doing a visual rebranding of your business, and now is a good time to incorporate stories.

Wherever you stand and whatever your goals, now is the time to put a plan in place so that you achieve your objectives.

Step #2 | Define your resources

You may be surprised to find you have more resources than you realize.

- If you have any staff, they may be interested in contributing stories. Who handles your customer service calls? No doubt there will be plenty of story material there, and perhaps a willing person who would like some variety in the job.
- Consider story contests for your staff. Quarterly, you could offer a prize for the best story. Topics could be the creative use of one of your products, a happy new

NOTES

NOTES

customer, a referred customer testimonial, or an upset customer turnaround.

- ♦ The same story contest can be used with your sales reps or agents. What stories do they have for overcoming objections or for explaining a new product?
- ♦ Don't forget to use company culture stories. If you have frequent new hires, then have your existing employees create stories that demonstrate company values, as Zappos does.

Step #3 | Develop story habits

Stories will not happen by themselves. Continuing to hone your story consciousness is the first step. Be aware of stories when you hear them. Be actively seeking stories in others. Be actively seeking story opportunities within your own business. Tell stories as often as you can.

Developing this level of commitment to stories, requires creating a new set of habits.

Desire alone is not enough. If desire and will power worked, we would all be thin, show up at the gym 5 times a week, have already learned French, reduced our dependence on our digital devices, or have achieved any of the other myriad resolutions we so optimistically make each new year.

Research has already proven that will power cannot create new habits. Habits are created by taking small steps, attaching a new habit to an existing behavior known as an anchor (or trigger), and by being motivated.

Your goal is to figure out how to anchor your new story habit into your existing routine so that it becomes a strong habit on its own.

One often used example is flossing your teeth. As you probably already brush your teeth (the anchor), it is easy to keep your spool of floss next to the toothbrush. Putting down the brush and then reaching for the floss becomes automatic. Your existing routine is one of the keys to developing a habit. The new habit needs to be simple and linked to an existing action that requires no thought or decision.

Develop strategies for dealing with:
- ♦ your star stories
- ♦ your supporting player stories
- ♦ your stage hands

As you progress, you will experience satisfaction and success with your story telling. Nothing helps establish a habit like success.

If you haven't given much thought to creating habits and need some ideas, please see the books mentioned in Chapter 10. There has been excellent research on habit formation in the last few years. There is no point trying the old ineffective, and self-defeating, will power method.

You may also be interested in Tiny Habits with BJ Fogg of Stanford University. BJ Fogg has created a free online program for teaching the Tiny Habits method. Sign up at www.tinyhabits.com and you will join a one-week program for learning about Tiny Habits. It's fun, enlightening, and free!

Step #4 | Work within your budget

This question always comes up: how do I do this when I have no money and no staff? When you are doing everything yourself, it may seem overwhelming to add even one more thing to the list. You are already working 60 hours a week trying to do sales, development, fulfillment, customer service, billing, inventory management, web site maintenance, and sweeping the floor. You are already worn out, how can you do more?

Adding more to your already impossibly long to-do list isn't the answer. The answer is threefold:
- ♦ Become more efficient in how you work
- ♦ Start small and build gradually
- ♦ As your budget grows (which is the point of all of this, isn't it?), hire physical or virtual staff to take the load off yourself.

NOTES

NOTES

_____

_____

_____

_____

_____

_____

_____

_____

_____

_____

_____

_____

_____

_____

_____

_____

_____

_____

_____

_____

_____

_____

_____

_____

_____

This allows you to hand off the routine or mundane tasks to others and lets you focus on building an Unstoppable Brand.

Become more efficient

Becoming more efficient in how you work is the cheapest and easiest way to get more done on a very tight budget. We can all be more efficient, and with so many technology tools available, you owe it to yourself to take advantage of these workhorses.

This isn't a book on work efficiency, but this is a good place to mention five great ways to get started on the road to efficiency.

- ♦ **Repurpose what you create.** If you write a blog post, could it become an ebook (or a chapter in an ebook), be turned into a podcast episode, or be reprinted in your newsletter? You don't want to send the same article out on every channel and annoy your followers, but always be looking for ways to transform something you have already created so it can have another life.

- ♦ **Automate repetitive tasks.** If you find that you are typing the same thing over and over, such as an answer to a question, a customer service response, or even a long name or email address, look into a text expander. I use Breevy Text Expander® on the PC and the built-in tools on the Mac®. You define the abbreviation and the text you want to be inserted. Every time you type the abbreviation, it is automatically replaced with the full text. You can use Breevy to replace words you frequently misspell or for full pages of text.

- ♦ **Record your thoughts.** Use voice recorders, either a physical recorder or a smartphone app, to take dictation. Dragon® Dictation is one such tool, but there are others, and they have all come a long way from the days you needed to train them to recognize your speech. I find my best ideas come in the shower, so I use AquaNotes® waterproof note pads to keep from losing these great, but fleeting, ideas.

Don't let good ideas float off into the ether; record them as they happen.

♦ **Get organized.** File your ideas, web sites, articles, PDFs, and audio files,etc. with Google Keep™ or Evernote®. Evernote has mobile apps for recording a message on your phone and filing it in the Evernote system. You can record notes up to 2 hours in length! Evernote can synch with all your devices for easy reference and updates.

♦ **Find affordable help.** Use one of the many online sources, such as elance.com, freelance.com, and the like. You can find people willing to work for surprisingly affordable rates. Also, check out your local high school or community college for students looking for small jobs. Try the local college for marketing students looking for experience in developing web sites or in conducting market research projects.

Start small and grow

We have covered quite a few topics in this book and you may be feeling overwhelmed. Relax. This is a journey, not a day trip. Start small with perhaps your core story. Keep looking for story ideas and fit your story crafting into those little windows of opportunity that we all have, such as while driving to work or waiting in line at the grocery store. Take 10 minutes in the morning to review one page of your web site and look for a story opportunity.

To keep the "go slow" method working, it is critical you have a schedule. Make a list of all the story opportunities and assign each to a date on your calendar. You must keep yourself accountable, or it will be too easy to abandon your story plan when some business emergency crops up.

Remember that building an Unstoppable Brand is a strategic effort. It will change how customers and employees view your business. This transformation won't happen by itself, and it cannot happen if it is considered as something to do when you have some free time. You must make time for this work.

Your Action List

Do not close this book without defining the next five things you WILL do. Each action item should result in real progress to a story-based brand.

Action #1

Action #2

Action #3

Action #4

Action #5

Stay in Touch

Please stay in touch!

Visit the book's web site:
www.unstoppablebrand.com

- Check out any corrections or additions to this book.
- Subscribe to the Story Alchemy newsletter on the web site.
- Send me your success stories, and I will publish them on the site, if you like.
- Send me any suggestions you have for improving this book.
- Let me know about local small businesses that are doing a great job of story telling.
- Send me your marketing stories so that I can share them with others.
- See announcements of Unstoppable Brand workshops.
- Let me know if you would like to schedule a workshop in your area.

Or, email me at
janet.wentworth@gmail.com

Most importantly, keep telling those stories!

Step #5 | Join a group

Look for some story-minded folks at your local chamber of commerce or business networking group. Start your own group if necessary. Be an evangelist for stories and attract others who see their value; you will be helping them and yourself!

Step #6 | List five things you can do now

The most important thing you can do is to make a list of five things you will do next to keep the story habit going. Post this list in prominent spots so you cannot forget. If possible, get someone to hold you accountable.

Step #7 | Keep it going

Working on your stories never ends, but one day you will realize that stories have become second nature to your marketing. You start to see story opportunities everywhere. This is the goal. When you have the story habit so ingrained that stories are as natural as a morning coffee or brushing your teeth, you have become a storyteller!

Remember, "Do or do not. There is no try."

Bring on the storytellers

A few months back I invited a friend to speak in front of my professional writing class. Santosh Jayaram is the quintessential Silicon Valley high-tech entrepreneur: tech-savvy, empirical, ferociously competitive, and a veteran of Google, Twitter, and a new start-up, Dabble. Afraid that he would simply run over my writing students, telling them to switch majors before it was too late, I asked him not to crush the kids' hopes any more than they already were.

Santosh said, "Are you kidding? English majors are exactly the people I'm looking for." He explained: Twenty years ago, if you wanted to start a company, you spent a month or so figuring out the product you wanted to build, then devoted the next 10 or 12 months to developing the prototype, tooling up, and getting into full production.

These days, he said, everything has been turned upside down. Most products now are virtual, such as iPhone apps. You don't build them so much as construct them from chunks of existing software code—and that work can be contracted out to hungry teams of programmers anywhere in the world, who can do it in a couple of weeks.

But to get to that point, he said, you must spend a year searching for that one undeveloped niche that you can capture. And you must also use that time to find angel or venture investment, establish strategic partners, convince talented people to take the risk and join your firm, explain your product to code writers and designers, and, most of all, begin to market to prospective major customers. And you have to do all of that without an actual product.

"And how do you do that?" Santosh asked."You tell stories." Stories, he said, about your product and how it will be used that are so vivid that your potential stakeholders imagine it already exists and is already part of their daily lives. Almost anything you can imagine you can now build, said Santosh, so the battleground in business has shifted from engineering, which everybody can do, to storytelling, for which many fewer people have real talent. "That's why I want to meet your English majors," he said.

Asked once what made his company special, Steve Jobs replied: "It's in Apple's DNA that technology alone is not enough — it's technology married with liberal arts, married with the humanities, that yields us the result that makes our heart sing."

**This story first appeared in *Santa Clara Magazine*, Winter 2013.
It was written by Michael S. Malone, author, journalist, television host, and adjunct professor in the Department of English at Santa Clara University.**

Your ideal customers are waiting for your story.

What will you say that makes their hearts sing?

How will your stories create Your Unstoppable Brand?

Visit our delicious.com page for all the web links mentioned in this book, plus many more useful resources.
www.delicious.com/unstoppablebrand

Visit the web site for this book where you will find updates, links to web resources on storytelling and marketing, how to sign up for the newsletter, and more.
www.unstoppablebrand.com

www.UnstoppableBrand.com

SAMPLE STORIES

The sample stories that follow are for you to read, enjoy, and analyze. They were selected because they illustrate many of the points discussed in the previous chapters and reflect a variety of writing styles.

This is not to say they are all perfect as standalone stories. These have been taken out of context. They might have been part of a book cover, one article in a series, part of a longer article, or a web page, and were written with that context in mind.

But being out of context does not detract from the stories themselves. Read through them and be alert for writing styles, word choices, visual layout, and clarity of message. Also watch for places you think they could be improved.

Perhaps some of them are stories that could be rewritten to apply to your business. For example, can you model John Jantsch's positioning story and create one as simple and powerful as his for your business?

Can you use Neal Gottlieb's story of sea salted caramel ice cream as a model for one of your product development stories?

Or, perhaps you have a relative like Uncle Hiromichi who could inspire a story of values, family tradition, and its impact on your business.

A few things to notice about each story are provided, but you are encouraged to provide your own analysis of each story. Who is the ideal customer for this story? Does the author make the best choices for all possible story elements? Can you do better? Is there something you think would improve the story?

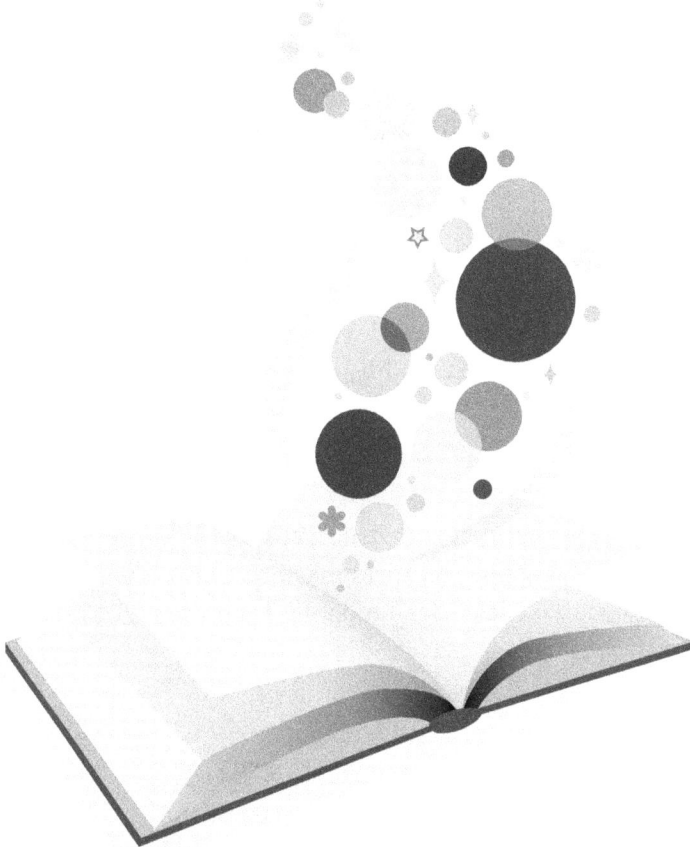

About the Power of PsychoTactics

By Sean D'Souza, Psychotactics

It all started with a copywriter called Leo Burnett

15+ years ago, fresh out of college with a degree in accounting (of all things) I joined an advertising agency called Leo Burnett.

There I "met" a man who had spent his lifetime in the hard trenches of communication and advertising. Few people have made more of an impression on me than the spirit of Leo Burnett himself. His determination (in the middle of the Great Depression) and his integrity shone through even though he'd been dead for many years.

From copywriting to cartoons

This opportunity of working with one of the best advertising agencies in the world took me on the heady road of copywriting, writing TV commercials (and learning how to do them in 5 seconds), graphic design, cartoons and web design. The underlying synchronicity was the constant search to find ways to communicate in the simplest, most effective manner.

Are you a psychologist?

No. But I understand a good deal about how customers think. Why they do what they do. Understanding the psychology of customers is what fascinates me most of all.

I read about 100 books or more a year, and listen extensively to audio tapes on learning while in the car (learned this from James C. Collins, Author of 'Good to Great' and from sales maestro, Brian Tracy). The knowledge contained in those audio tapes and books, when meshed with my own, helps me to give readers, workshop participants and clients a unique perspective on business. Psychologist I may not be, but psycho I can be :)

Dad was a teacher, mum was a teacher, grandma too...

All the information I provide through articles, teleclasses, etc., is distilled and structured. It's a family thing. Teaching runs in my blood. I was taught early in life that teaching requires mastery. Only when you have total control over the subject, can you simplify it and make it understandable. Then there's dedication, focus and discipline.

Up at 4

It's a normal working day, when the clock strikes 4. That's why if you write to me (DON'T CALL ...you'll wake up everyone else!), you'll often get responses at weird hours. It's the best part of the morning and it helps me focus on the nitty gritties of the human brain and why it does what it does. My parents always woke up early and that has stuck. What has also stuck is the ability to pass on that knowledge freely.

The fountain of knowledge flows freely. Jump in and frolic in it!

Things to Notice in this Story

Compelling introduction

The opening reference to Leo Burnett will get anyone who is familiar with the legendary advertising genius Leo Burnett wanting to know how Sean is connected to Leo. Sean then immediately moves us into his experience with the Leo Burnett Agency which gives him great credibility. At this point, the reader is hooked and willing to read more.

Use of subheads to make the text less daunting

Notice the use of subheads. They divide the story into five sections which makes this longer story less of a chore to read. They help structure the story, but are not just factual phrases to introduce a new topic, they are interesting bits that help move the story along and keep the reader intrigued. "From copywriting to cartoons" sets the stage for his career progression. But, "Are you a psychologist?" Asks a question most people will be asking as they read, and this gives Sean a chance to address this possible objection up-front. "Dad was a teacher, Mum was a teacher, grandma, too . ." Adds a personal touch and gives Sean credibility as a member of a teaching family who saw good teaching methods in action. The last subhead "Up at 4" is a bit off the wall, and yet it reflects Sean's quirky style and moves us from his history to his approach today. These are not just subheads, but carefully planned devices to move us through the story.

Variety of sentence structures

Sentences vary in length from one word to forty. He answers the subhead "Are you a psychologist"?" with a simple "No." That is all that is needed, and it adds a dramatic touch.

Lack of strict chronology

This story starts with Sean's initial job, gives a bit of his life at the agency (but does not get bogged down in the details), answers an objection about his background in psychology, than goes to his early family upbringing, and then zooms ahead to today and getting up at 4 am.

Introduction of values

The story enables Sean to demonstrate his values of simple, effective communication, hard work, and desire for mastery.

Reflection of his Sage archetype

Sean is a Sage who provides valuable marketing, business, and productivity insights to his followers. But he also has a great sense of humor as illustrated by his cartoons, which are used on his web site and in his book. By presenting himself as a "psycho Sage" he appeals to a very specific ideal customer: one who values solid advice, wants someone who walks the talk, appreciates a Sage who is always learning (the 100 books a year habit), is generous with information (many free reports and one-on-one help in the forum), and yet has a charming, quirky style.

This is a great example of the founder's story including his passion and purpose. It also is very true to his generous spirit and dedication to his craft. Sean is an author, teacher, and speaker, as well as creator of an vibrant global online community of small business owners. You can read more from Sean at www.psychotactics.com.

Why I Wrote a Book

By Kerry Rego, Kerry Rego Consulting

I know it sounds odd, a social media consultant writing a dead tree book.

As long as I've been working in social media, I have received requests for DVDs or other recorded materials from my clients and seminar attendees. Social media changes from minute to minute, day by day, so I took my time in selecting a subject that would stand the test of time.

Watching people, listening to their concerns, and tracking trends for years gave me my answer. Technologies change and brands get sold. What stays the same is us, for our whole lives. What I know to be true is that you spend your whole life developing your character and reputation and today, one post, one video, one stupid mistake, can be your ruin when it's online. While many of my client requests are for Facebook page building, LinkedIn understanding, social media strategies, and measuring marketing channels, I knew they needed more. When I started adding reputation management and personal branding to my services, my clients were shocked at what we found. They felt uneducated and helpless to change what others saw on search engines.

There's a ton of marketing and business focused social media resources available. What I don't see much of is easy to understand information for business owners, schools, parents, children, and people of all walks of life on how to navigate the web, understand what's happening, stay safe, and build a positive route for success. This book is a start.

This is my higher calling:

Educate people on the truth of the situation and how it affects them.

Assure them there are ways to be proactive and assertive.

Empower them with action items they can perform to protect themselves and their loved ones.

This book is not about social media strategy specifically, though I do cover it. This book is for everyone to use, understand, and learn what tools are available to control how they are seen online when they aren't around to speak for themselves.

I know not everyone likes social media or wants to use it. Many aren't ready yet and may never be but that doesn't mean they don't deserve the information should they desire it. I wrote a paperback book because I want to reach as many people as possible, particularly those that aren't constantly attached to technological devices, this book is first and foremost for them. And for those that prefer digital books, it's also available in Kindle format and soon in iBook. You can get your copy here.

Plain and simple, this subject is too important to neglect. Knowledge is power.

Things to Notice in this Story

Compelling but quick introduction

Kerry's book is about online reputation management, yet she starts by addressing dead tree books. This is a good hook to get the reader's attention and then she quickly segues into the changing landscape of social media.

Good purpose story for her ideal reader

Kerry explains her work with individuals and businesses, and their relationship with social media. This book is not for the techie who is on every platform from Twitter to Facebook to Tumblr. It is not for those creating a social media strategy. It speaks right to the ideal reader: what the average web user can do to understand how her reputation is being built on the web, how to stay safe, and what tools are available for her to use to make this happen.

Strong message

Yes, there is no hiding on the web. Even my father, who lived a quiet, introverted life, and who died in 2000 can be found with a Google search. My aunt actually emailed me a few weeks ago when she found him in a Google search and was terrified of how this information got out "there." Kerry's message that we all need to be aware of how our information is being made public and what we can do to protect our reputations is necessary, especially for her target audience, such as people like my aunt.

Clarity

The explanation of why Kerry wrote this book is simple and clear. Clarity is always the most important element in your writing. Yes, we strive for well-crafted sentences and drama. But, if the reader misses the point, why bother? It is clear from this book introduction why Kerry wrote the book, who should read it, and why it is important. What more can you ask?

Kerry Rego is a social media / technology trainer and keynote speaker based in Santa Rosa, CA. She has just published her first book, *What You Don't Know About Social Media CAN Hurt You.* **Read more about her at www.kerryregoconsulting.com.**

The Story of Sea Salted Caramel

By Neal Gottlieb, Founder of Three Twins Ice Cream

For the real scoop on Three Twins' flavors, we went straight to the source: Founding Twin Neal Gottlieb. Here's what he says about our sweet and sassy superstar, Sea Salted Caramel.

Salted caramel is the new black. It's everywhere: in ice cream, on cupcakes and in your nonfat, shade-grown, songbird-safe goat's milk molten lava hot caramel latte. But, one place it hadn't been was in the form of an inconceivably delicious, certified organic ice cream. And as it turns out, creating an organic salted caramel ice cream isn't as easy as apple pie (though the two do go together quite well).

Finding an appropriate organic caramel really proved to be a challenge. I found a few folks who were making organic caramel, and although their hearts were in the right places, the caramel was by no means flavorful enough to make an ice cream that was unquestionably delicious. So I set forth to do better for you, my loyal reader. And for the children.

After locating a company that made caramel for various applications, I was enthused to learn that they would work with us to develop a certified organic caramel to use as the foundation of our Sea Salted Caramel ice cream. When I got the first samples, I was less than impressed.

It wasn't that the samples were bad; in fact, they were quite tasty. It was the ingredients that were the problem, and two ingredients in particular. The first ingredient that I wanted to take outside and have words with was "natural flavor." Though I was raised in New Jersey, which is home to a good portion of the chemical companies that make the country's natural and artificial flavors, I don't see a place for such things in my ice cream or anything else that I eat.

Flavors are things that are trying to taste like things but that don't really taste like the thing that they're trying to taste like. The result is poor approximations and worse aftertastes. I use only real things in my ice cream, not things trying to taste like things. It is a simple rule with little to no room for debate, and it has decidedly delicious consequences.

The other ingredient that was banished was something with a name I can't even remember. It contained four syllables over two words, and I can't really be bothered to look it up. It's dead to me. The purpose of this ingredient, I was told, was to act as a buffer. I don't know what that means and neither did my sales rep, so I demanded that he leave it out.

I am happy to say that, after several test batches, the caramel company nailed it. They gave us a caramel with a clean ingredient statement and the balance of a rich caramel taste, with a tease of sea salt that allows this kid to play in the big leagues. This is not some little leaguer playing left out. This is a Hall-of-Famer in the making. And unlike some that you'll find in Cooperstown, you won't find asterisks next to this one due to the addition of synthetic stuff.

Fun fact: I love this flavor so much that I decided to take the unprecedented step of releasing it not only in pints, but also in single-serve cups. At the same time. You are welcome.

Things to Notice in this Story

Good illustration of conflict

The struggle to find just the right ingredients for an all-organic ice cream is not an epic, Star Wars-type drama. It is the simple, but determined struggle to find the right organic ice cream recipe. Most of us have this type of somewhat commonplace struggle, and it is up to us to write our story so that it reflects our important goal. Neil does a good job by weaving in the details of the various trials, the idea that the ice cream had to be good for children, and his determined quest for the best.

Follows the story arc

Easy to follow story of the state of salted caramel flavours, the search for quality sea salted caramel ice cream, the many failures that used unacceptable ingredients, the climax when the right recipe was developed, and then the resolution of releasing the new flavor in pints and single-serve cups. This story follows the chronological arc, and yet isn't a boring recitation of events due to the writing style of the author.

Clever use of baseball comparison

The unexpected introduction of the baseball analogy at the end adds a surprising twist and yet fits so well with the back-to-simpler-times archetype of this brand. Rather than ending with just "we finally got the flavor nailed," Neil really makes it memorable with the mention of Cooperstown and the National Baseball Hall of Fame.

This is a very effective use of an analogy as it adds just enough of a twist, but does not bog the entire story down with trying to keep the analogy going. It is easy to think of an analogy and then force weave it into the entire story. Sometimes more is less.

Aligned with archetype

Three Twins is a good Innocent archetype as it tries to bring back the "gold old days" of real ice cream made with no artificial ingredients. The simple logo and writing style fit with this archetype. As you read this story, you notice the company appreciation for real things, for "creating ice cream that is good for the children," and of course, for that all-American pastime of baseball.

Neil Gottlieb is the Founding Twin of Three Twins Ice Cream. In 2005, the company began as a one-man show in San Rafael, California but is now a national brand sold in over 35 states. You can read all of his stories about the company, the ice cream, and the delivery truck, Carl at www.threetwinsicecream.com.

Uncle Hiromichi Survives the Tsunami

By Boku Kodama, Center Manager, Renaissance Marin

It's been nearly two years since my Uncle Hiromichi was disrupted by the most devastating earthquake to ever hit Japan. He lived and worked in Sendai, at the heart of where the tsunami hit shore. Over 20,000 people died in that disaster.

Uncle Hiromichi was home that day attending to his garden when he heard the loudest, most violent sound imaginable. He rose quickly eastward in the direction of the rumbling. Suddenly, the ocean rose - devouring everything in its path; bringing hell into view.

Without thinking he ran into his house and quickly climbed to the second floor. Just as he reached the top stairs, the entire house slammed sideways with a shattering sound so loud that it made Uncle Hiromichi go deaf for a few seconds. Dazed, hurting and not knowing which way was up, he had enough instinct to grab onto a metal bar leading to the attic. He held on for dear life.

Then, the unthinkable happened. His home, now ripped from its foundation, was launched like a missile in chaos as if to be sucked into the clutches of a black hole. The deafening power of the tsunami made it hard to think. This is the end, he thought.

In his mind's eye, Uncle Hiromichi saw his home smashing against a concrete building or a hillside. But he gathered himself. "I'm not dead yet and until then, I must 'gambaro' (fight to stay alive)."

It must have felt never-ending but in less than 15 minutes, it came to a crashing halt, somewhere eight kilometers away in a farm field pummeled against so many other indistinguishable objects.

We called him but there were no answers. For five days, we had no idea what had happened to him. We knew the likelihood of his demise was probable. But on the sixth day, he phoned!

"Uncle Hiromichi, you are one lucky guy!" I said. Yes, he acknowledged in his usual calm voice, "but I wasn't sure I would make it." For four days in the snow, he survived by constantly scavenging through the debris for food, shelter and anything to stay warm. When he was found by rescuers, he was bruised but unbroken in body or spirit.

"How did you stay strong?" I asked.
Do you still study the Bushido?" he responded. "I guess not enough," I confessed.

"It's what kept me going." The Bushido is translated as the Code of the Samurai (Warrior). It's a lifestyle based on honor, honesty, harmony and ethics. "Are you still teaching business?"

I knew what he was getting at. He once told me that business reflects the soul of its creator and that one cannot separate one's beliefs from that of the business. When you have a great business, you get up enthused and burn to make something better every day.

If there's a spark, and you believe in the goodness of what you do, then getting the right kind of entrepreneurship training can lead to a life known as the Genius of the And: doing something you love and making a living from it.

Things to Notice in this Story

Captures interest with human interest story

This story was the introduction to an email message promoting a business workshop. Everyone on the list is familiar with the Renaissance Center and also with Boku, the author. They would all be immediately interested in the story of his uncle. If the story was about an unfamiliar person and the tsunami, it might not have had the same attraction.

Story based on current news

Tying a story into some current event is often an effective way to get attention, especially when it is such a global news story. Boku's story nicely brings that global tragedy down to a very personal level, creating an irresistible pull for us to keep reading.

Powerful descriptions

"Bringing hell into view," "smashing against a concrete building," "farm field pummeled," and many other descriptors really let us experience the ordeal Uncle Hiromichi suffered. Review the story again to see all the places you feel an especially strong emotional pull.

Dramatic contrasts

Notice the changing drama: we start in a peaceful garden, then come violent sounds, the scramble up the stairs, hanging on for dear life. The tension continues, and then suddenly we get a phone call. Now he is calm, having recovered from this near-death ordeal. We learn of the Bushido and how this code of honor, honesty, harmony, and ethics enabled him to survive Japan's most devastating earthquake. Then, suddenly, "are you still teaching business?" and we are back in the moment. This entire story is one wild ride of emotional and physical contrasts.

Use of a disconnect

Notice the skillful switch from discussing the tsunami survival story to "Are you still teaching business?" There is no subhead, no lead-in, just the quick pivot to the reason for the email. If this story appeals to you and you feel a connection with "Genius of the And," you know you are the ideal customer for this entrepreneurship training. There is no need for a list of features and benefits or a section on "who should take this course." This is also done very quickly. The majority of the story is about Uncle Hiromichi and the tsunami. Only the last two paragraphs are about the entrepreneurship, and only the last paragraph is about a training program. When you have a great story meeting an ideal customer you don't need the hard sell.

Boku Kodama is a serial entrepreneur and Center Manager for Renaissance Marin. He has 40 years experience as an entrepreneur, having started ten for-profit and nine non-profit businesses. His entrepreneurship programs are unconventional and designed for the 21st century economy using collaboration, creativity, and referral marketing.

My Positioning Story

By John Jantsch, Founder of Duct Tape Marketing

This is the story that illustrates how you want the market to perceive your brand. Of course, perception is partly a goal and partly a measurement because some things are out of your hands. A true positioning story, however, is one that authentically captures your purpose in action – it's how purpose is packaged in a way that allows the intended market to connect.

And, the best positioning stories can usually be summed up in one word.

Early on in my marketing consulting business I was invited to be part of a pitch for a very large piece of business. It was a national firm that wanted to hire a national ad agency, but also include a local marketing support company for the local branch.

The New York ad agency sent five people, all clad in black head to toe and armed with a 100-page deck filled with research and recommendations.

When it came time for me to offer my two cents I said something like – I don't know, why don't we just talk to some of your current customers? The meeting ended and the next day the VP that was conducting the search called and said he wanted me to do the entire project without the New York ad agency. To this day I can hear him say why – "you were the only one that said anything that was practical."

And that's part of my positioning story.

Things to Notice in this Story

Illustrates the writer's values

This is a simple story that shows John in action. The reader clearly sees that John is not swayed by high-powered clients or agencies. He stays true to his core of practical marketing. Any potential client would immediately know if he were right for them. A business that needed an impressive Madison Avenue firm would go elsewhere. One looking for down-to-earth, common sense advice would be immediately attracted to John.

Short and clear

Often the best stories are very short. They waste no time with unnecessary details. This one gets right to the point. A quick explanation of the meeting, his offer, and the client's response. By staying short, the story is more powerful.

Just enough detail

Although it is short, the story does have illuminating details. The phrases "all clad in black head to toe" and "armed with 100-page deck" say it all. He didn't need to describe the room, the table, each of the players, etc. We can easily create the scene in our heads from these few details, as we have all been in a situation similar to this. The result is we can each make this story our own, and yet it still conveys John's message.

Casual style matches his archetype

John Jantsch is all about being an approachable and practical Sage. This story clearly illustrates this with his response "I don't know, why don't we just talk to some of your current customers?" No pretense, no trying to sound like a big ad agency. He knows exactly who he is and the value he brings. There is no need for him to dress it up.

States his authentic brand promise

If you follow John Jantsch you know he really delivers on practical marketing ideas. He is able to cut through all the hype and broken promises of marketing advice to the essence of what a small business owner needs to do for successful marketing. If you have heard him speak, you can hear his voice in this story. This is John—pure, simple, and practical!

John Jantsch is a marketing consultant, speaker, and author of *Duct Tape Marketing, The Commitment Engine,* and *The Referral Engine,* and is the founder of the Duct Tape Marketing Consultant Network. The original article can be found at:
www.ducttapemarketing.com/blog/2011/09/21/four-stories-every-business-must-build/

Why Black Tea Needs to be Steeped with Boiling Water

By Marcus Stout, Owner, Golden Moon Tea

Back in college I wasn't the most "sophisticated" person. I lived in a dorm that had a TV, two beds, my roommate's giant hamster poster (that is a story within itself) and a microwave.

I also ate very basic foods and, by that, I mean I ate whatever was cheapest. So, like most college kids, I ate Ramen all the time. Each meal costs about $0.30 and it takes about 3 minutes to make. At the time it was a no brainer.

But when I look back, Ramen is pretty tricky when you don't have a kettle or stove. At first I would just pour really hot water into the bowl and let it sit for about 10 minutes. I wasn't too bright back then so as you can imagine, this did not work at all. The noodles came out stiff as a board and quite disgusting.

The next time I made Ramen I popped the water and noodles in the microwave and let it cook for a few minutes. This worked like a charm. The reason it worked is the water actually boiled when I put it in the microwave. The problem I had with the hot water method was that the water needed to be boiling. It is the only way that the Ramen Noodles would actually cook.

Black tea is the same way. If you don't use water that is hot enough, then you will never get it to taste right no matter how long you steep it for.

The flavors lie in flavanoids

Black tea has certain chemical compounds, or flavanoids, that green and white teas do not have. These compounds are not released unless the water temperature is near boiling.

It is these flavanoids that give black tea its unique flavor

Scientists actually made a black tea beverage in a lab without using any tea at all. They combined 15 amino acids, 14 flavonol-glycosides, 8 flavan-3-ols, 5 theaflavins, 5 organic acids, 3 sugars and caffeine in their "natural" concentrations.

And the chemical concoction actually tasted the same as regular black tea

A lot of those flavanoids that the chemists used to make the black tea cannot be extracted at temperatures below boiling. Similar to the Ramen, no matter what you do it will not taste right.

But why doesn't green tea need boiling water?

That is a complicated question. However, in the most basic sense it is because green tea is not fermented as long as black tea. It is in this fermentation process that black tea produces these extra flavanoids that need the boiling water to extract.

Summary

While this has been a lot of scientific mumbo jumbo, the key to remember is that black tea will not taste right unless you use boiling water. While it won't turn out crunchy and disgusting like undercooked Ramen, it will lack the flavor and astringency that make it such a great beverage.

Things to Notice in this Story

Closing ties back to the opening
Marcus starts off with his college days and Ramen noodle eating (something so many former college students can relate to). Then he deftly refers back to the Ramen noodles in the closing paragraph.

Simple analogy of Ramen to black tea
Ramen noodles seem easy enough to make and so does tea: just add boiling water. But, as Marcus points out, neither is as easy as you think! He brings in a discussion of flavonoids, amino acids, and other technical elements, and this might be too technical for some. Adding the analogy to Ramen noodles keeps us on track and not lost in the chemistry.

Liberal use of subheads
The subheads create an outline of the article. You can get a good idea of the contents of the article just by scanning the subheads. This is especially important for online articles, as people often just scan through. If your subheads are interesting, they may stop and read the entire article.

The use of a summary
Calling out a "summary" will not work in an oral story (you will need to be a bit more subtle), but is a good idea in an article. Sometimes people try to be too clever with their writing, and this cleverness may interfere with the message. In Marcus' story, he clearly states the conclusion so no one will miss the point.

Simple facts become an appealing blog post
Marcus uses his blog as a way to educate his followers. He could have just given the facts about green and black tea, and when boiling water is needed. But most of us would quickly forget the distinction. By using an analogy to cooking Ramen noodles, and making it more interesting with pertinent details about his college dorm routine, he makes it more memorable. This is an effective approach when you don't have a full story for your message but can find an analogy that has the story elements.

Marcus Stout is the owner of Golden Moon Tea in Bristow, VA. Marcus is passionate about food, but especially about tea. Visit his web site www.goldenmoontea.com to read his personal passion story as well as the stories about his teas.

The Great Chef and The Failing Restaurant

By Robert Bruce, VP of Marketing, Copybloggere

When the Head Chef dramatically walked out in the middle of Friday night service, a Sous Chef found herself in charge of the well-known and respected Manhattan restaurant.

In the following months, though she was very competent, and was working day and night, the restaurant's reputation began to decline.

Fearing for her position, she made drastic changes to the menu. Then, a week later, she did so again. She reconsidered her seafood supplier. She negotiated with the General Manager for updated uniforms for the entire waitstaff. She replaced the tablecloths.

Despite these efforts, more and more patrons were walking out her door, shaking their heads in disappointment.

After a particularly bad weekend, she admitted that she could not see clearly the problems her restaurant faced, that she needed to somehow start over.

Without telling anyone, she snuck out of the restaurant, and began shadowing a prominent Chef in his neighboring kitchen several nights a week.

He was an aging culinary genius, and he didn't like to talk.

So, she stood next to him chopping, rolling, grilling, and boiling. As the nights passed, she became consumed with the Chef's technique, with his preparation, his orderliness.

Though she learned much, she could not find the secret, the one thing that would make the difference for her own dying restaurant. She continued to sweat, and observe, and worry.

Several weeks later — fearing that her current course of action was also futile — she thanked the great Chef, removed her apron, and turned to leave his kitchen.

"Ingredients," he whispered.

"What was that? I'm sorry?" she said.

"Ingredients. You don't respect them."

"How … what do you mean? I'm buying the best ingredients I can find. In fact, you and I share many of the same suppliers. I drive down to the farmer's market every week to pick the finest produce available, by hand …"

"That's not your problem," he said, dropping a handful of diced onions into a bowl.

"Well then, what the hell is my problem!?"

"Arrogance."

"Excuse me?" she said.

"You want to make something breathtaking, something unforgettable, a plate that will send your patrons into fits of ecstasy," he said.

"Yes, yes I do. And what's wrong with that?"

"What you fail to see is that your ingredients are already breathtaking," he said.

She waited.

"A great Chef learns to restrain herself, to respect good ingredients. She works very hard to simply avoid screwing them up."

He'd moved on to the whole pig he was breaking down, his blade passing through its shoulder effortlessly.

"There are a thousand ways to deface a beautiful tomato," he whispered to himself, now gently holding the pig's head in his hand.

She stood in the doorway of the kitchen for a moment, speechless. Then she turned, and walked quickly back to her own restaurant.

Robert Bruce is Copyblogger Media's Chief Copywriter and its Resident Recluse. You can read more from him, as well as get great copywriting articles, at www.copyblogger.com.

Things to Notice in this Story

Visual layout to create drama

Notice how almost every paragraph is a single sentence. This visual layout helps slow down the pace of the story. Without this layout you could just read through at a fast clip and completely miss the emotion of this story. You need this visual brake so that you feel the inner tension of the chef and let the plot elements and message be revealed in its dramatic fashion.

Strong message

The author could have simply stated that any chef (or wannabee chef) must respect her ingredients. But that would not be nearly as memorable as this story. How could you forget the chef's torment at her failing business and her search for the answer. How can you forget the master chef's handling of the pig?

The introduction of the pig butchering into the story, makes the simple beauty of the tomato so striking.

Use of dialogue

Rather than a narrator telling us what happened, the use of the main characters' dialogue makes the story come alive. Also, the dialogue contributes to the story's pacing, as we have to go through the entire encounter and do not just get a quick recap. This story requires the use of dialogue for its drama.

Conflict is physical and mental

Notice that there is the physical struggle (working day and night, following the master chef, dialogue) plus the internal struggle of the failing chef. For some stories, the conflict is tilted to one type of conflict over the other, but it may be that a combination will improve your story.

Skillful story arc

This story follows the strict chronology of the events but is never boring due to the use of dialogue, conflict, visual layout, and language choices.

RESOURCES

The following are books I have read and found useful in working with clients and in writing this book. Basic writers' resources should be owned by every aspiring story writer. They are critical if you are doing your own writing and will be publishing your work on your web site, in your brochures, and elsewhere. The other books listed will provide more depth to topics such as branding and storytelling, ideal customers, archetypes, and writing techniques than we were able to cover in this book.

Basic Writers' Resources

The Chicago Manual of Style: *The Essential Guide for Writers, Editors, and Publishers.* University of Chicago Press. Sixteenth Edition. 2010.

> An authoritative guide to writing style, grammar, and punctuation. No writer should be without this volume or another of equal reputation.

Oxford American Writer's Thesaurus. Compiled by Christine A. Lindberg. Oxford University Press. 2008.

> Another must-have for writers. Use this volume to find the right word and to find alternatives to words you may be overusing. Use it to eradicate couch-potato words in your writing.

On Writing Well: *The Classic Guide to Writing Nonfiction.* William Zinsser. Harper Perennial. 2006.

> Readable guide to writing nonfiction. Many chapters are on topics such as interviews, writing a memoir, and humor writing, that may not be of interest to the business marketer. But this book is such a trove of writing wisdom, it deserves to be read by everyone.

Eats, Shoots and Leaves: *The Zero Tolerance Approach to Punctuation.* Lynne Turss. Gotham. 2008.

> Who knew punctuation could be fun? Who knew punctuation could be a matter of life and death? Now you must read this book to find out why.

Storytelling

Believe Me: *Why Your Vision, Brand, and Leadership Need a Bigger Story*. Michael Margolis. Get Storied Press. 2009.
> A storytelling manifesto of change makers and innovators—and storytellers.

Story Proof: *The Science Behind the Startling Power of Story*. Kendall Haven. Libraries Unlimited. 2007.
> Excellent introduction to the research on stories and brain development. Haven provides the proof that stories are an effective teaching and learning tool.

The Story Factor: *Inspiration, Influence, and Persuasion Through the Art of Storytelling*. Annette Simmons. Basic Books. 2006.
> A classic book in the storytelling field. A book every aspiring storyteller should read.

On the Origin of Stories: *Evolution, Cognition, and Fiction*. Brian Boyd. The Belknap Press of Harvard University Press. 2010.
> A thorough and scholarly work on the evolutionary origins of story, and how it has contributed to human survival and progress. Discussions include Homer's *Odyssey* and Dr. Seuss' *Horton Hears a Who*!

Lead with a Story: *A Guide to Crafting Business Narratives that Captivate, Convince and Inspire*. Paul Smith. AMACOM. 2012.
> How to use a story within an organization to define culture and values, engender creativity and innovation, foster collaboration, provide coaching, and lead change.

Your Ideal Customer

Resonate: *Present Visual Stories that Transform Audiences*. Nancy Duarte. John Wiley and Sons, Inc. 2010.
> This is a book about doing presentations rather than stories. However, the opening chapter on resonance, and later chapters on myths, movies, heroes, and other topics are important for story creators.

The Brain Audit: *Why Customers Buy and Why They Don't*. Sean D'Souza. Psychotactics Ltd. 2009.
> Good book for all marketers on understanding what prevents people from making buying decisions. One chapter explains how to identify ideal customers.

Archetypes

Online Resources

www.marketingideas101.com/branding-101-discover-your-brand-archetype-quiz/
Take this free, easy, online quiz and you will receive an email with the results.

www.proprofs.com/quiz-school/story.php?title=brand-archetypes#
Twelve questions about your company. It will immediately return your archetype.

www.inspectorinsight.com/archetypes/
Review of the 12 major archetypes. Interesting comments, examples, and quotes.

Brand Metaphors Kit: Brand Metaphors 101
www.fortyagency.com/resources/brand-metaphors
A free downloadable 10-page PDF of branding and metaphors.

Books

The Hero and the Outlaws: *Building Extraordinary Brands Through the Power of Archetypes*. Margaret Mark & Carol S. Pearson. McGraw-Hill. 2001.
If you only read one book on archetypes, make it this one. Thorough explanation of the 12 main archetypes with clear examples and ways to apply archetypes to your business.

Archetypes in Branding: *A Toolkit for Creatives and Strategists*. Margaret Pott Hartwell and Joshua C. Chen. HOW Books. 2012.
Beautifully produced book that presents 60 archetypes in an easy to understand format.

What Story Are You Living? A *Self-Improvement Guide for Discovering the Unconscious Influences that Drive Your Life Story*. Carol S. Pearson and Hugh K. Mark. Center for Application of Psychological Type, Inc. 2007.
This book and the included Pearson-Marr Archetype Indicator Assessment are designed for individual, not business, assessment. However, it can be useful for many business owners, especially solo entrepreneurs with a business that is an extension of their personal characteristics and passions.

Blogs on Writing

Copyblogger: www.copyblogger.com/

Daily Writing Tips: www.dailywritingtips.com

Karen Thackston: www.marketingwords.com/blog/

Writing Techniques

Bird by Bird: Some Instructions on Writing and Life. Anne Lamott. Anchor Books. 1995.
Insights into the writer's world with advice for anyone entering there. Funny and wise and written as only Anne Lamott can.

Wired for Story: *The Writer's Guide to Using Brain Science to Hook Readers from the Very First Sentence.* Lisa Cron. 10 Speed Press. 2012.
Twelve cognitive "secrets" with explanation of how to use them for story writing. The book covers more advanced topics, such as character development, that may be beyond your needs, but this book is an important contribution to the science and craft of story writing.

Follow the Story: *How to Write Successful Nonfiction.* James B. Stewart. TouchStone Books. 1998.
An advanced book on writing nonfiction that will be of interest to those looking to develop their writing skills and write longer, more complex stories.

Branding through Stories

www.zapposinsights.com/culture-book

Get a free copy of this book written by Zappos employees. Full of photos, quotes, and employee stories. Not everyone is right for the Zappos culture, but it won't take long to figure that out when looking at this book.

Storytelling: *Branding in Practice.* Klaus Fog et al. Springer. 2010.
One of the original books on story-based brands. Examples are large brands, but it does offer good comparisons to fairy tales and other accessible ways to create stories.

Stories that Sell: *Turn Satisfied Customers into Your Most Powerful Sales and Marketing Assets.* Casey Hibbard. AIM Publishers. 2009.

> This book focuses on using stories in the sales cycle. It offers very specific techniques for shortening your sales cycle and getting prospects to say yes.

Winning the Story Wars: *Why Those Who Tell—and Live —the Best Stories Will Rule the Future.* Jonah Sachs. Harvard Business Review Press. 2012.

> Good explanation of why stories have become so critical now. It also offers some practical advice, although most of the advice is more useful for a large company with marketing resources, than for a small business. Still a worthwhile read.

StoryBranding: *Creating Standout Brands through the Power of Story.* Jim Signorelli. Greenleaf Bookgroup Press. 2012.

> Good book on why you need a story-based brand and exercises on how to get there. It may be more useful for someone with a marketing background than a small business owner trying to do it all with no marketing expertise. I especially liked the I AM Your Customer exercise. Everyone can benefit from doing this exercise.

Tell Me a Story: *Storytelling to Create Impact Brands.* Jan Bierman. Rare Design Ltd. 2012.

> At only 31 pages long (on my Kindle), this ebook is a quick read, but it is a nice introduction to storytelling and includes a few great stories

Building Good Writing Habits

Switch: *How to Change Things When Change Is Hard.* Chip Heath and Dan Heath. Crown Publishers. 2010.

> Another wonderful and useful read from the Heath Brothers. The book covers how our rational minds and our emotional minds are in conflict, usually giving the edge to the emotional mind. But we can overcome this tension and get the results we really seek.

Rewire Your Brain: *Think Your Way to a Better Life.* John B Arden, PhD. Wiley. 2010.

> Using the latest from neuroscience research, learn ways to rewire your brain to improve your mood, improve your memory, and change your habits. Where we once thought the brain was hardwired, we now know it is soft wired by experiences. We can now use this knowledge to improve our lives—and learn to make story-writing a life-long habit.

The Power of Habit: *Why We do What We do in Life and in Business.* Charles Duhigg. Random House. 2012.

> A thorough discussion of how habits are formed, and how we can use that knowledge to create better habits without resorting to will power as our only tool. Lots of great stories of people who changed their habits for your inspiration.

Too Important to Ignore

Primal Branding: *Create Zealots for Your Brand, Your Company, and Your Future.*
Patrick Hanlon. Free Press. 2011.
> Excellent companion to story telling as it covers the important ways you can support your stories through words, visuals, rituals, icons, and other primal methods.

Made to Stick: *Why Some Ideas Survive and Others Die.* Chip Heath and Dan Heath.
Random House. 2006.
> As a business person, you are always trying to communicate ideas to your prospects, partners, and customers. This books gives you a strategy for making sure that these ideas stick in the minds of your intended target. Of course, story is one of the strategies. An enjoyable read.

All Marketers Are Liars: *The Power of Telling Authentic Stories in a Low-Trust World.*
Seth Godin. Portfolio. 2000.
> Godin was one of the early evangelists for using stories in marketing. Learn why brands such as Fiji Water are winning the marketing wars through their use of stories. Typical Seth Godin pulls-no-punches writing style.

Brainfluence: *100 Ways to Persuade and Convince.* Roger Dooley. John Wiley and Sons. 2011.
> How neuroscience and behavior research can explain consumers decisions patterns, and how you can apply this to improve your marketing. Goes beyond storytelling to discuss pricing, loyalty rewards, and other marketing efforts.

Unconscious Branding: *How Neuroscience Can Empower (and Inspire) Marketing.*
Douglas Von Pros. Palgrave Macmillan. 2012.
> Another book that presents current findings in neuromarketing.
>
> The author's basic thesis is that the majority of our decision are made by our unconscious. He explains how consumer research is wasted asking people what they prefer or what they would do. Those decision are made by our unconscious minds, not our rational minds.

The Art of Storytelling, *From Parents to Professionals.* Professor Hannah B. Harvey,
East Tennessee State University. The Great Courses. www.thegreatcourses.com
> The Great Courses offers DVD, audio, and online streaming courses on a wide variety of topics. This course is for parents and professional storytellers, but if you are thinking of using oral stories as part of your marketing, you will find this course valuable.

Visit our delicious.com page for all the web links mentioned in this book, plus many more useful resources.
www.delicious.com/unstoppablebrand

Visit the web site for this book where you will find updates, links to web resources on storytelling and marketing, how to sign up for the newsletter, and more.
www.unstoppablebrand.com

www.UnstoppableBrand.com

www.ingramcontent.com/pod-product-compliance
Lightning Source LLC
Chambersburg PA
CBHW051222200326
41519CB00025B/7218